Morning Meetings

FOR SPECIAL EDUCATION CLASSROOMS

Morning Meetings

FOR SPECIAL EDUCATION CLASSROOMS

101 Fun Ideas, Creative Activities and Adaptable Techniques

FELICIA DURDEN, ED.D.

Published in the United States by:
Ulysses Press
P.O. Box 3440
Berkeley, CA 94703
www.ulyssespress.com

ISBN13: 978-1-61243-681-4
Library of Congress Control Number: 2016957540

Printed in the United States
10 9 8 7 6 5 4 3 2 1

Acquisitions editor: Casie Vogel
Managing editor: Claire Chun
Editor: Renee Rutledge
Proofreader: Shayna Keyles
Front cover design: Rebecca Lown
Interior design and layout: what!design @ whtaweb.com
Cover artwork: cover and chapter graphics © AnnRas/shutterstock.com
Interior artwork: see page 246

CONTENTS

CHAPTER 4: STRATEGIES FOR SKILLS DEVELOPMENT IN ENGLISH LANGUAGE ARTS AND SOCIAL STUDIES 97

INTRODUCTION

Congratulations on starting, renewing, or tweaking your journey using morning meetings in your elementary special needs classroom. The morning meeting method is a framework to use to start your day of learning. It involves bringing your students together as a community to learn. This book will provide instructional strategies to use during your morning meeting time.

Morning meetings enhance the learning experiences of your students and provide you the opportunity to work on goals; teach important social, emotional, and problem-solving skills; and informally assess students. I used the morning meeting method for over 10 years when I was a classroom teacher. It was the most essential routine of my day because of the long-lasting rewards it afforded me and my students.

As a school administrator, I've found the morning meeting to be an excellent strategy, which has proven to help build a culture and climate that is supportive and inclusive for the special needs population. When I walk through classrooms, I'm amazed to see students engaged in authentic inclusive learning. Study after study has concluded that morning meetings not only support building an inclusive culture and climate, but also serve as a catalyst for student academic success. I could not imagine teaching without utilizing the morning meeting method.

I will provide information about diverse strategies for using morning meetings to work with students with special needs. The strategies illustrate how the morning meeting routine helps support an inclusive learning environment and different learning targets. I will then share specific techniques on how to implement the routine in your elementary classroom. This book contains 100 activities that can be implemented during your morning meeting routine. Each activity is followed by a Common Core English Language Arts (ELA) Anchor Standard or Mathematical Practice or Next Generation Science Standard. The standards listed indicate the standard that addresses the instructional practices in the strategy listed.

Chapter I
WHY MORNING MEETINGS?

Often, teachers feel that morning meetings are a waste of instructional time. Actually, the contrary is true. When students start their day on a high note they will have fewer behavioral issues, which are real time-wasters.

I have seen the morning meeting implemented in special needs classrooms across the United States. It can be utilized in self-contained models for students with varied needs. It can also be used in all grade levels. One of the underlying benefits of the morning meeting routine is that it provides a sense of belonging for students. When students join the morning meeting, they are asked to participate in the learning process; this immediately makes them feel like they belong and have an important role in their learning process. It also helps them feel like part of something bigger than themselves. They start to see that the classroom is theirs and that the learning revolves around all students.

This is an important leveling tool that teachers can benefit from when they implement the morning meeting routine in their classrooms. The days of the teacher being the sage on the stage, or the ruler of the roost, are over. The sage on the stage premise promotes the idea of the teacher being the dominant figure in the classroom who takes sole responsibility for what happens there. The paradigm has shifted in the twenty-first century classroom, where we now see the importance of having students guide the instructional process and be active participants in their own learning. With this idea in practice, students are part of the discussion, have classroom jobs, vote on classroom issues, and help and guide one another in their learning. All of these twenty-first century skills are highlighted in the morning meeting routine.

Today's classrooms are inclusive places of learning, where teachers serve as facilitators of the learning.

Teacher as Facilitator of Learning

As a facilitator, your job is to make the learning process accessible and stress-free for your learners. Facilitation means you provide students with the tools to be problem solvers and self-dependent learners. It does not mean making the curriculum unchallenging or providing low levels of rigor in the classroom. Students should be able to meet the expectation levels that you set for them. As the facilitator of the morning meeting, your job is to provide kids with the tools they need to maneuver the school day by starting it off with a positive routine.

What Constitutes a Good Classroom Environment for Learning?

Classroom environment has been shown to be pivotal in student achievement. Students thrive in classroom environments that are safe, inclusive, orderly, attractive, and comfortable.

Safe Classroom Environment

A safe classroom environment is one in which students feel physically, emotionally, and socially secure. These classroom environments have a positive tone, and students feel that the adults in the classroom care about them and their needs.

Physical safety is accomplished by establishing classroom rules and expectations of behavior. When you model the appropriate ways to solve conflict, talk to others, and disagree, you help students learn the skills they need to ensure they feel safe and secure.

Emotional safety is accomplished by ensuring students don't endure undue emotional stress. Today many of our students come to class with a lot of outside issues from home. These issues can trickle into the classroom and cause emotional stress. As a teacher, you can curtail emotional stress by getting to know your students and having authentic conversations with them about their lives. This book will outline several getting-to-know-you strategies that you can easily implement during your morning meeting routine to help ease emotional stress.

Social safety is also important in the classroom. Students need to feel free, when appropriate, to interact with their classmates, teachers, and other adults inside and outside of the classroom. Social safety is threatened when students do not feel that they have a voice or that they belong to the group. To combat these fears and develop social safety, students need opportunities to talk to their classmates and build teams. In the upcoming chapters, you will learn numerous team-building, social networking, and classroom inclusion strategies to help students feel socially accepted and enjoy contributing, which are necessary parts of the classroom environment.

The morning meeting offers a plethora of opportunities to help build a sense of security and safety in the classroom. Taking the time to get to know your students and having them take time to get to know one another will accomplish this.

Inclusive Classroom Environment

An inclusive classroom environment is one in which every student has a part in the learning process and is considered an equal contributor to the learning. Inclusive classroom environments have been shown to foster greater student academic growth than non-inclusive classrooms. "Inclusive" refers to making the learning connected to student interest and providing opportunities for students to engage. In an inclusive environment, teachers see to it that all students participate.

Taking Student Interest into Account

Students have been shown to learn at greater levels when they are exposed to content that has meaning for them. Think about your own learning experiences. Did you do better in courses that you had an interest in? I know I did better in courses that interested me. I'd be far more engaged in a sewing class than in an auto mechanics course. These two examples may be far out there, but are they? With the morning meeting routine, you can find ways to take student surveys on activities or themes that your students have interest in. There are many strategies shared in the book on how to use trade books and literature to teach concepts and skills. When selecting the books or passages that you want to share, think inclusively and provide materials that your students will have a special connection with.

Orderly Classroom Environment

Chaos reaps chaos in the classroom and in any work environment. Students do not thrive in a chaotic environment and, in fact, are more likely to act out aggressively or become introverted when they are victim to chaotic learning environments.

An orderly classroom is pivotal if you are going to use the morning meeting method there. An orderly environment will ensure that your morning meeting routine flows, and is well planned and executed. The upcoming chapters share numerous strategies regarding ways to set up your morning meeting area and to run your morning meetings to create an orderly routine that is predictable for students.

Attractive Classroom Environment

An attractive classroom helps students acclimate to their learning environment. Do not feel pressured to make your classroom look like something out of a designer magazine, but do take the time to spruce up your room and make it attractive and warm. Think about the colors that you are using in your classroom. Red, yellow, and other very bright colors can make students agitated and distracted. Try to use colors from nature, like green, blue, and brown in your morning meeting area. These colors have been associated with creating a sense of calm and well-being in the classroom. Also, watch the clutter. We all have so much stuff these days. Although it is wonderful that we have so many resources to provide for our students' needs, it's important to make sure that you organize those materials in a way that ensures your classroom remains orderly and clean. This will help cut down on student anxiety and stress, which you want to avoid. Students learn a lot about their own orderliness from the school environment.

Comfortable Classroom Environment

Having a learning environment that is comfortable is another important step in preparing to implement the morning meeting routine in your classroom. By comfortable I refer not only to physical comfort by having the classroom clean and orderly, but also social comfort by allowing students the ability to express their thoughts and feelings without distractions. Students should feel comfortable during morning meeting to ask questions, share opinions, sing, dance, and act silly. This book is full of exciting strategies you can use to enhance the fun and comfort your students will thrive on.

The Responsive Classroom Philosophy

One of the founding principles behind the morning meeting method is the responsive classroom philosophy. The responsive classroom philosophy is based on the link between academic achievement and social and emotional learning. The responsive classroom philosophy was developed in 1981 by a group of educators who saw the need to embrace social and emotional learning to meet the needs of students.

The four components of the responsive classroom method are engaging academics, positive community, effective management, and developmental awareness.

Engaging Academics. When teachers develop engaging academics, they take into account student interests when creating assignments. This is accomplished during the morning meeting when teachers provide opportunities for student choice and student input in the topics that are presented.

Positive Community. The morning meeting is all about students. Without students there would be no morning meeting. This is very significant in building a positive learning community.

Positive communities are ones where students have voice and feel safe and secure in their learning environment. During morning meeting, students work with different partners to share the learning experience and build positive relationships. Students also have a clear feeling of belonging to something that matters.

Effective Management. One of the most important things to remember before implementing the morning meeting is that you must have structures in place to maintain order. The morning meeting is a time to engage in conversation and explore different learning activities. This cannot be well-executed without maintaining a sense of order and routine.

Developmental Awareness. As I have reiterated, morning meeting is for and about kids. When working with students with special needs, it is imperative the activities are developmentally appropriate and manageable so that all learners can engage in the activities. Each strategy has a suggested modification and a tip so that all students have the opportunity to participate. This is the most important tenet of the responsive classroom philosophy.

Morning meetings are the building blocks of the responsive classroom philosophy. They have their own morning meeting framework that includes many of the same structures that are presented in this book. One additional practice that the responsive classroom model supports is implementing a closing meeting, which I will discuss in the final chapter of the book as a way to keep your morning meeting fresh and alive.

Why Focus on Social and Emotional Learning?

The activities and structure of the morning meeting have a direct correlation with social and emotional learning, which have been linked with easing anxiety for students with special needs.

Students tend to be happier and more ready to learn when they are in classrooms that use the morning meeting. Often, children with special needs suffer from anxiety or have problems with transitioning throughout the day. We have found that when these kids are in classrooms that use morning meetings, they are less agitated and have more success. In a research study titled "Efficacy of the Responsive Classroom Approach: Results from a Three-Year, Longitudinal Randomized Controlled Trial," researchers found that schools that focus on social and emotional learning have higher academic results than those that do not. Research also has indicated that students with special needs do much better when this model is implemented in their program.

It works, because we all need to feel accepted and welcome. Morning meetings serve as a way to provide a sense of connection for your students. Often, students with special needs require time to assimilate to their surroundings. Research has found that when kids feel connected, they are far more successful in their learning routines. The morning meeting is an awesome way to bridge this gap.

Special Needs Populations and Morning Meetings

Having a morning routine that includes coming together as a class to discuss the schedule for the day and teach essential skills is a great way to create an inclusive learning environment for your students. Students with special needs are especially in need of structured environments that are predictable and well-managed. They also thrive in environments that foster inclusion and celebrate diversity.

There are numerous benefits in using the morning meeting routine with your special needs students. In this section, I will discuss specific ways to ensure students with disabilities are given an opportunity to thrive during the morning meeting routine.

Cognitive Deficits. Students with cognitive delays benefit from the morning meeting routine because it is a time when they can be successful in the classroom. They are able to participate in the singing and movement activities as well as many of the other routines.

Processing Deficits. Students with processing deficits are typically classified as having learning disabilities. These students benefit from the morning meeting routine because they will receive intense instruction that is spiraled and differentiated. When you design your morning meeting mini lessons, you can target the lessons to focus on specific deficits that your students need to master.

Sensory Deficits. The small setting of the morning meeting routine is beneficial to students with sensory deficits because they will be able to hear and see the material that is being presented. They will have the opportunity to sit close to the teacher and be actively involved in the learning process. I share some strategies that teach students sign language and social cues, like reading body language. These are very important skills that students with sensory deficits will find beneficial.

Emotional and Behavioral Concerns. Many students with social and behavioral concerns lack social cuing skills and do not know how to properly interact with others. The morning meeting routine serves as a wonderful place to teach these important social skills in a group setting. Students will practice their listening skills along with how to take turns when speaking. They will also have opportunities to rate their day and discuss how they are feeling. These are just some of the many opportunities the morning meeting routine will offer to assist students in building their social and emotional intelligence, which is so important for students with emotional and behavioral concerns.

Physical and Health Problems. A benefit of using the morning routine with students with physical and health problems is that they will be able to participate in the group learning and not have to be held back in any way. All of the activities in the morning meeting routine, including each of the strategies in this book, can be differentiated to accommodate the physical needs of all students.

Autism

Students with autism will find the morning meeting routine a perfect opportunity to work on communication skills. During the morning meeting, students work in groups and discuss ideas with a neighbor. These are key skills that will be beneficial for students with autism. Another important skill that students with autism will practice during morning meeting is taking turns when talking or sharing information. This is a skill that many children with autism lack. Structures will be set up to ensure students are aware of what taking turns looks like, and they will be able to practice this important skill in a group setting where immediate feedback occurs.

Gifted and Talented

Students classified as gifted and talented will have the opportunity to showcase their talents during morning meeting. It is the perfect venue for students to lead discussions and take part in engaging research projects. It also serves as a perfect structure to support peer-to-peer interaction, which will be helpful for your gifted and talented populations.

Improved Academic Performance

There have been numerous studies that have concluded that when students work in inclusive environments, their achievement soars. Research study after research study has concluded that students who are in classrooms that support integration of content, differentiate instruction, foster independence, and promote a safe learning environment perform better academically than those in classrooms that don't have these characteristics. The morning meeting routine does all of these things on a daily basis. Students are introduced to and taught multiple skills in an integrative method. They are taught to work independently and modeled the social skills they will need to be successful in school and beyond. They experience a safe learning environment where they have ownership and feel safe to take risks. They take part in making the rules and enforcing them.

Where Do You Begin?

The morning meeting ritual helps fulfill students' need to feel like they belong, be safe, and most importantly, start the day in fun way. I have been in education for over 15 years. During this time, I have seen a lot of programs come and go. One thing remains: kids are kids, and we need to ensure they feel supported and happy when they are in our care.

I have used the morning meeting method in my regular education and special education classrooms, and the results speak for themselves. Kids feel welcome, are able to share what they know, and have a sense of well-being that sets the tone for the day. Seeing children smiling and eager to share their ideas is proof enough for me that the method is worth using. I have seen children come out of their shell and begin to talk and interact with others when using the method. I have watched children smile from ear to ear when their friends validate their ideas. I have witnessed shy children going over to high-five friends with confidence and joy. In the next few pages, I will share some strategies, pitfalls, and ideas so that you too can start utilizing this powerful method with your students.

Following are four steps you need to take to get started right away with morning meetings.

Set Up a Morning Meeting Area in Your Classroom

Where will you hold your morning meeting? The area needs to be roomy enough so each student has room to write if necessary and talk to a neighbor without being too crowded. Many teachers set up their morning meeting on a large carpet that is facing a whiteboard or bulletin board. You will need to decide which area in your classroom will best facilitate this.

Some teachers like to have their students sit in a circle during morning meeting. Some like to have the kids in chairs, and others have the students sit on the floor. This, again, is entirely up to you. You might want to try it a few ways and see what seating arrangement works best for your kids.

The key is to have an area where everyone feels comfortable and has plenty of space to work.

The teacher setup for morning meeting is very important. You will be doing some direct instruction, so you want to have access to a whiteboard, chalkboard, or something similar so you can write information to share with students when necessary. You will also share the calendar and use charts to display information. Keep all this in mind when deciding on the area you want to set up for your morning meeting. Most classrooms have a few areas with whiteboard space, so you can typically find a corner of the room that will serve as your morning meeting area that will not interfere with your main teaching area for the bulk of the day. I suggest having a distinctive area for your morning meetings that is not part of your classroom teaching area. This will help make the morning meeting area special.

Plan Your Morning Meeting Routine

Take the time to think about how your morning meeting routine is going to flow. Remember there is no right or wrong way to run your morning meetings. The key is to create a routine that you can stick with and that is conducive to student learning.

There are a few things to keep in mind when developing your routine. You want to have time for students to greet each other, go over the schedule for the day, and work on a skill. These are the three essential things you will want to include in your morning meeting each day.

There are a lot of different things that you can do during morning meeting. Singing, reading stories, and writing are all important and should be included in your morning meetings throughout the week, but keep in mind that you can alternate your morning meeting routine so that you can sprinkle in different content and activities for your students' benefit.

In several classrooms I have visited, teachers have singing time on Monday and Friday to start and end the week with a fun activity. Think about the activities you want to alternate to best meet your classroom needs.

Sample Schedule

Greeting. Start your morning meeting with a greeting. This is very important as it sets the stage and helps everyone loosen up. You can have kids greet one another by shaking hands, exchanging high fives, or sharing another form of greeting. The goal is to make sure everyone is greeted with a friendly hello.

Calendar. Share the calendar and discuss any important events.

Song/story. Engage students in a song or story to help set the tone for the day. The story or song chosen can support the main learning objective of the day.

Content teaching. This is where you will teach or reinforce your teaching point for the day. You can choose from any of the strategies shared in the book to teach during this time.

Group activity/individual work time. This is where you will have the group work together to complete a task.

Review. Review the major objective of the lesson or skill taught during the session. This will enable students to process they key ideas of the session.

Closing routine. End your morning meeting with a closing routine. This routine may include celebrating the students' effort during morning meeting, singing a closing song, or having kids do a chant to get them started for the day. The closing routine is important because it ends your morning meeting in a structured way each day.

Plan the Time Slot

Most teachers have a 30- to 45-minute morning meeting routine. Yours will depend on your schedule. One of the issues teachers report is that they may have special classes like physical education, art, or music that interfere with their morning routine. Work with school administration to get your specials scheduled around your morning meeting timeframe. It is important to start the day with morning meeting. You may start 30 minutes later on certain days of the week, but I advocate for having the morning meeting be the first thing you do each day. This helps set your tone for the rest of the school day.

As you implement your morning meeting, you will soon be able to determine how much time you need to get through all the necessary components. You don't want the meeting to be too short or too long. Keep tweaking until you get it just right for you and your students.

Get All Necessary Supplies

You will need several supplies to ensure your morning meeting is successful. Make sure to secure the following:

- Calendar with numbers
- Chart stand
- Pointer
- Pens
- Markers
- Index cards

The following are optional items you may consider using based on your preferences and classroom needs:

- Large carpet for students to sit on
- Dry erase boards
- Pocket chart
- Big bookstand
- Timer

Chapter 2
STRATEGIES FOR BUILDING COMMUNITY

The morning meeting is a community-building activity. When you have a strong classroom community, you build trust and relationships. Both are so important when working with special needs children. In order to build community, you must start with a set of rules and expectations that your community agrees to abide by. Have the children help create and enforce the rules to allow them to internalize the expectations.

This chapter is filled with strategies to support team building. Your kids will work on understanding differences, finding commonalities, understanding rules and procedures, and the list goes on.

I. Teaching Rules and Expectations

MATERIALS NEEDED

- Chart paper
- Marker
- Chart paper with a T-chart of an eye and ear drawn on it

RATIONALE: Students often have IEP goals that revolve around following directions. Understanding the necessity for classroom rules is important for developing a good social climate, order, and structure in their learning environment. There has been so much research on how kids feel disequilibrium when they are in chaotic environments. This activity will help reinforce an important life skill that they will need to be successful in life. Students will continually have to follow rules, and learning about them during morning meeting makes the task less intimidating.

PROCEDURE

o Start the lesson by asking kids to talk about why rules are important.

o Take any and all suggestions and record them on chart paper.

o Explain to students that you will be working on the rules and expectations for morning meeting. In your explanation, be very explicit regarding the importance of following rules.

o Emphasize the fact that following rules helps ensure your morning meetings run smoothly.

o Have a T-chart available with a picture of an eye and an ear. This chart will be used to record what the desired behavior looks and sounds like.

- Have a predetermined set of rules for morning meeting time. These rules can include taking turns when speaking, sitting on the carpet quietly, raising your hand when you have a question, etc.

- As you introduce each rule, talk to kids about what the rule looks and sounds like. Record the responses on the T-chart.

- Take the time to model what each rule would look and sound like. For example, sitting at attention looks like your legs are crossed and your hands are on your lap. It sounds like silence as you are sitting quietly.

- Have students model the behavioral expectations for each rule.

- Reinforce these rules daily. You will want to go over them for as long as necessary for the kids to really understand what your expectations are.

- Post the rules in a prominent area so you and the kids can refer to them.

MODIFICATIONS: If you have students who need extra help with modeling the rules, you can help them by sitting with them one on one and modeling the expectations.

Use visual representations of the rules to help your kids see what the rules are.

Consider recording kids following the rules and sharing the recordings with students to reinforce the behavior.

TIPS: Teaching rules and expectations for morning meeting is the first step in ensuring your morning meeting routine goes off without a hitch. Remember that the time spent teaching these rules is worthwhile; don't skimp on it. Make it a priority and you will be happy in the future.

ANCHOR STANDARD ADDRESSED

CCSS.ELA-LITERACY.CCRA.SL.I — Prepare for and participate effectively in a range of conversations and collaborations with diverse partners, building on others' ideas and expressing their own clearly and persuasively.

2. Classroom Jobs

MATERIALS NEEDED

- Note pad
- Pen
- List of classroom jobs (pictures can be used to help students visualize the job role)

RATIONALE: The morning meeting serves as an excellent venue to reinforce social skills. The social skills of responsibility and organization are very important in the special needs classroom. Having a classroom job helps students build ownership and responsibility for the care of the classroom. It also provides accountability for ensuring the classroom environment is safe and orderly.

Classroom jobs help students learn to care for their environment. This important life skill helps build community and leadership. Students should have assigned jobs in the classroom to help support their social and emotional development.

PROCEDURE

- Let students know that each week, you will assign students to serve as classroom helpers.
- Share the list of classroom jobs that students will be able to serve in (have a predetermined list of jobs ready).
- Go over each job and explain the duties related to the position.
- Ask students to share which jobs they think they would like to perform.
- Listen to their conversations and take note. This information can help you decide where to initially place students.
- Assign the students for the job(s) that they will perform.
- Explain that each week you will rotate the jobs, so everyone has a chance to serve in each role.

o Post the classroom jobs chart in a prominent area so you and the kids can see who is responsible for each job.

MODIFICATIONS: If students will need assistance completing a job assignment, be sure to have modifications in place so they can serve in their post.

Have an aide or other student help a child complete their job tasks if necessary.

⚑ **TIPS:** To avoid student competition over classroom jobs, be sure to rotate the responsibilities frequently. Do not punish kids by not allowing them to have a classroom job. Give each child the opportunity to serve in these roles to build their self-esteem.

ANCHOR STANDARD ADDRESSED

CCSS.ELA-LITERACY.CCRA.SL.1 — Prepare for and participate effectively in a range of conversations and collaborations with diverse partners, building on others' ideas and expressing their own clearly and persuasively.

3. Picture Schedules

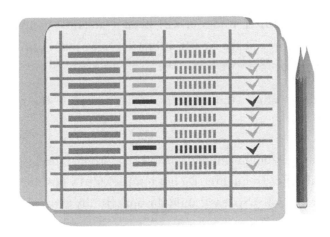

MATERIALS NEEDED
- Picture schedule cards
- Chart with Velcro to move the schedule cards

RATIONALE: Picture schedules can help students maintain a sense of well-being in the classroom. They are often used in IEPs to provide scaffolds for students who need visual cues. They serve as a great tool to share what will be expected during the day, such as a fire drill or a special class, like PE or music, and to understand that there is a clear end to each activity. Students often face anxiety when there is any change in their routine. The picture schedule serves as a cue of a coming change and can help ease this anxiety. I have sat in on numerous IEP meetings where picture schedules have assisted students with autism, providing a sense of security for them as they move through the day.

PROCEDURE
- Review the schedule for the day.
- Have the picture cards already posted to the schedule board.
- Let students know what the day's activities are.

o As each task is completed, turn the cards over or remove them from the schedule.

MODIFICATIONS: Some students may need an individual schedule to keep at their desk.

You can put both words and pictures on the schedule, depending on the students' level of need.

TIPS: Be sure to choose pictures that are easily recognizable for the students. This will help ensure there is no confusion regarding what task or activity is being represented. Also, make sure to update the schedule daily. Often there are changes made and you want to make sure you indicate the changes to prevent any angst.

ANCHOR STANDARD ADDRESSED

CCSS.ELA-LITERACY.CCRA.SL.I — Prepare for and participate effectively in a range of conversations and collaborations with diverse partners, building on others' ideas and expressing their own clearly and persuasively.

4. Practice, Practice, Practice

RATIONALE: Never underestimate the power of practicing the behaviors that you want to see exhibited in your classroom. As students go through life, they will find many times when they will have to perfect their behaviors to meet the necessary standards. Practicing the morning meeting routine to get out the kinks will be necessary as you continue to build this structure into your classroom. You will need to pick specific parts of the routine that need tweaking in order to change behaviors and progress.

PROCEDURE

o After spending some time using the morning routine, pick a day to practice some of the areas of the routine that need to be perfected.

o Let students know that you will practice some of the steps of the morning routine that need to be improved.

o Talk about professional sports players who practice as an example of how to get better at what they do.

o Be overly explicit and dramatic when you practice the necessary steps of the morning meeting that need tweaking.

o Once you have practiced, ask the kids to rate their performance.

o Let students know that you will continue to practice as necessary until they have the steps down to perfection.

MODIFICATIONS: There may only be individual students who need to practice particular parts of the morning routine. If this is the case, set aside time to work with kids individually.

☛ **TIPS:** Be sure to maintain a positive and upbeat demeanor as you practice the skills. You want to ensure that students see the importance of practicing but don't feel deflated or overly criticized.

ANCHOR STANDARD ADDRESSED

CCSS.ELA-LITERACY.CCRA.SL.I — Prepare for and participate effectively in a range of conversations and collaborations with diverse partners, building on others' ideas and expressing their own clearly and persuasively.

5. All About Me

MATERIALS NEEDED

- Student copies of All About Me sheet (page 236)
- Markers
- Chart paper

RATIONALE: Providing students with an opportunity to share about themselves builds student self-esteem. This activity provides a structure to use for students to learn to share ideas which is an important social skill.

PROCEDURE

- ○ Prep for the activity by copying the All About Me sheet template on a piece of chart paper.

- ○ Have markers readily available to use when you complete your model.

- ○ Gather students together for morning meeting. Explain that today they will be completing an activity that will help you learn more about each other.

o Tell students that in order to learn more about each other they will be completing an All About Me sheet. Explain that the sheet will provide information about their favorite things to do and will help the class see how they are alike.

o Model by filling out an All About Me sheet with your own information.

o Show students the All About Me sheet that they will be completing.

o Remind them that they can use your sample to help them fill out their own sheet.

o Release students to work on the sheet.

o Once students have completed their sheets, have them share them and post them in the room to help build community and celebrate their efforts.

MODIFICATIONS: If you have an instructional assistant, have them help students fill out their sheets.

Have students draw pictures to represent their information if this accommodation is necessary.

Have students dictate their answers to an adult or other student.

If working with older students, adapt the sheet to include more probing questions. For example, "What is your favorite subject? How do you like to spend the weekend? Who do you admire most and why?" Instead of having the student draw a portrait, they can write an important fact about themselves.

🖝 **TIPS:** Completing activities like the All About Me sheet helps students feel self-worth and acceptance. It is important to include all student ideas on the sheet to validate their ideas.

CCSS.ELA-LITERACY.CCRA.W.3 — Write narratives to develop real or imagined experiences or events using effective technique, well-chosen details, and well-structured event sequences.

6. Personal Timeline

MATERIALS NEEDED

- Preprepared timeline listing important events from your life
- Timeline handout for parents (page 237)

RATIONALE: Understanding where you fit in the world is a critical life and social skill. This activity helps students gain perspective on how their lives unfold and how important they are. It also celebrates their unique contributions to the classroom. Each year this activity is a big hit as kids proudly share their timelines.

PROCEDURE

- Let students know that you have completed a timeline.
- Explain that a timeline is used to list events in chronological order.
- Share your preprepared timeline with the class.
- Let students know that they will be creating their own timelines to share with the class.
- Send a note to parents with the timeline sheet.
- Once parents have returned the pictures and dates on the timeline, create a few minutes for each student to share their timeline with the class.
- Post the timelines in a prominent place to celebrate student diversity.
- This activity can be a team builder at the beginning of your morning meeting routine.

MODIFICATIONS: You may have students that need individual help with completing this timeline. Be sure to identify them and have a plan in place to assist them.

🏴 **TIPS:** Maintain a positive and upbeat demeanor as you share the timeline and instructions for creating one. Creating timelines allows students to practice their sequencing skills. Use your timeline instruction as a time to talk about sequencing and order.

CCSS.ELA-LITERACY.CCRA.SL.I — Prepare for and participate effectively in a range of conversations and collaborations with diverse partners, building on others' ideas and expressing their own clearly and persuasively.

CCSS.ELA-LITERACY.CCRA.SL.4 — Present information, findings, and supporting evidence such that listeners can follow the line of reasoning and the organization, development, and style are appropriate to the task, purpose, and audience.

CCSS.ELA-LITERACY.CCRA.SL.5 — Make strategic use of digital media and visual displays of data to express information and enhance understanding of presentations.

7. What We Have in Common

MATERIALS NEEDED

- Chart paper
- Markers
- Student copies of What We Have in Common template (page 238)

RATIONALE: Finding commonalites in group settings is important for students with special needs. It helps to create and foster a community that is inclusive and supportive. This activity will enable your students to begin to see how much they share in common with their fellow classmates. It can help build student esteem and develop tolerance and acceptance.

PROCEDURE

- Ask students if they know what the word "common" means.

- Create a chart titled "What We Have in Common."

- Let students know that you will ask some questions and see how much the class shares in common.

- Pass out copies of the What We Have In Common sheet and markers, and have the students answer the questions with the teacher's help.

- Once the sheets have been completed, go over the responses and record the things the students have in common.

- Ask students what they think about how much they have in common.

o End by sharing how much you all share in common.

o Ask students to share something interesting they learned about their classmates from the activity.

MODIFICATIONS: Depending on the academic and cognitive level of your students, you can modify the activity to meet their individual needs. Modifications may include completing the task with the teacher or having the student work with a partner to complete the task.

TIPS: This activity is very powerful when you ensure that students are able to share their responses. Make sure to build in enough time for discussion when doing this activity. It works best when completed in one teaching session. You may have to cut back on some other activities to accomplish this.

ANCHOR STANDARDS ADDRESSED

CCSS.ELA-LITERACY.CCRA.SL.I — Prepare for and participate effectively in a range of conversations and collaborations with diverse partners, building on others' ideas and expressing their own clearly and persuasively.

CCSS.ELA-LITERACY.CCRA.W.4 — Produce clear and coherent writing in which the development, organization, and style are appropriate to task, purpose, and audience.

8. Celebrate Differences

MATERIALS NEEDED

- Chart paper
- Markers
- Student copies of Unique Me worksheet (page 238)

RATIONALE: This activity allows students to see how they differ from others. It provides an opportunity to begin to compare and contrast, which is an important skill they will need in varied subject areas.

PROCEDURE

- Let students know that they will be learning how they are different.
- Ask students if they know what the word "different" means.
- Take any and all contributions.
- Explain what the word "different" means and write the definition on a chart or board.
- Show students a picture of an elephant and a picture of a giraffe.
- Ask students to talk with a partner about how the two animals are different.
- Bring students back together and have volunteers share what they discussed with their partners.
- Record what the students share on your chart.
- Tell students that they are now going to work with a partner and discover how they are different from one another.

o Go over the Unique Me worksheet. Each partner will mark an X in either the Same or Different column, depending on whether or not the student and their partner have the same or different responses to the questions.

o Provide time for students to work on their sheet with their partners.

o Monitor and provide assistance as needed as students work.

o Bring partners back together.

o Have students share what they discovered about how they are different from their partner with the class.

o End the lesson by discussing how important it is that we all have differences.

o Explain that our differences are what make your classroom so strong. If we were all the same, things would be boring, but because we all have unique gifts and strengths, your class is complete.

MODIFICATIONS: Provide assistance with filling out the Unique Me worksheet with students who need this scaffold.

ANCHOR STANDARDS ADDRESSED

CCSS.ELA-LITERACY.CCRA.SL.1 — Prepare for and participate effectively in a range of conversations and collaborations with diverse partners, building on others' ideas and expressing their own clearly and persuasively.

CCSS.ELA-LITERACY.CCRA.SL.4 — Present information, findings, and supporting evidence such that listeners can follow the line of reasoning and the organization, development, and style are appropriate to the task, purpose, and audience.

9. Cultural Exchange

MATERIALS NEEDED

- Projector and prepared Power Point slide presentation about your upbringing
- Chart paper
- Markers
- Cultural Exchange worksheet (page 239)

RATIONALE: Finding commonalities in a group setting is important for students with special needs. It helps to create and foster a community that is inclusive and supportive. This activity will enable your students to begin to see how much they share in common with their fellow classmates. This is an important idea to reinforce in the classroom as it helps to build an inclusive classroom culture.

PROCEDURE

o You will share a Power Point slide presentation that includes information about your upbringing. Include the following slides in your PPT: Slide 1— Early Life (On this slide, share your birth name and date of birth); Slide 2— Traditions (Share special family and cultural traditions); and Slide 3—Fun and Festivities (Share special food your family enjoys and celebrations you take part in).

o Model the process for the student presentations.

o Share the cultural exchange worksheet and let students know they can use the questions on the worksheet to help them complete their slide presentation.

o Give the students time to work on their slide presentations.

o Allow students time to practice their presentation before presenting it to the class.

o Share student presentations.

o Consider allowing students to bring in some treats to share.

MODIFICATIONS: Depending on the age and grade level, parent help may be necessary to complete the activity.

If you do not have technology to create and share the PPT presentation, the activity can be completed using a poster board.

Some students may need assistance with sharing their presentation. Have someone readily available to assist if necessary.

TIPS: Ensure that each child has the opportunity to participate in this activity. It is very important that each child gets to share their family culture and traditions.

ANCHOR STANDARDS ADDRESSED

CCSS.ELA-LITERACY.CCRA.SL.I — Prepare for and participate effectively in a range of conversations and collaborations with diverse partners, building on others' ideas and expressing their own clearly and persuasively.

CCSS.ELA-LITERACY.CCRA.SL.4 — Present information, findings, and supporting evidence such that listeners can follow the line of reasoning and the organization, development, and style are appropriate to the task, purpose, and audience.

CCSS.ELA-LITERACY.CCRA.SL.5 — Make strategic use of digital media and visual displays of data to express information and enhance understanding of presentations.

10. Building Teams

MATERIALS NEEDED
- Chart paper
- Markers

RATIONALE: Building a sense of team cohesion is important in the special needs classroom. Students need to feel like they are part of the group, and team-building activities are a wonderful way to foster this.

PROCEDURE
- Start by letting students know that they are part of a classroom community and team.
- Explain that teams work together to get things done.
- Ask students to share any teams they have been a part of.
- Take any and all examples and write them on a chart.
- Ask students how they think team players act. Write their ideas on chart paper. Be sure to bring out things like working together, supporting others, etc.
- Tell students that they will be coming up with a classroom team name and team cheer today.

- Start by asking students to brainstorm team names. Record them on a board.

- Once you have a few names chosen, vote as a class on your team name.

- Next, solicit student ideas of an appropriate cheer to represent the class.

- Have kids share their team cheers and vote on the one the class wants to adopt.

- Each day, share your team cheer to bring the class together.

MODIFICATIONS: If students are having trouble coming up with a team name or team cheer, be sure to have a few already ready to share for them.

If students need assistance with sharing their cheers, be sure to have plans in place to assist.

☛ **TIPS:** The team cheer can get a little noisy and rambunctious. To combat, this be sure to model appropriate voice tone for the team cheer.

You may also want to change the team cheer periodically to keep it fresh and alive.

ANCHOR STANDARD ADDRESSED

CCSS.ELA-LITERACY.CCRA.SL.1 — Prepare for and participate effectively in a range of conversations and collaborations with diverse partners, building on others' ideas and expressing their own clearly and persuasively.

II. Games and Contests

MATERIALS NEEDED

- Chart with review of game rules
- Beach ball or other large ball

RATIONALE: Having a game-like atmosphere during morning meeting helps students become actively engaged in the process. Engaged students learn and retain more information. The following strategies can be used to make any activity more engaging.

PREP

Create a chart with the following game rules.

- Teacher asks a question.
- Think about the answer inside your head.
- The ball is tossed around until the teacher says stop.
- The person with the ball has to answer the question.
- If he or she answers incorrectly, the ball is tossed again until the teachers says stop.
- The person with the ball gets a chance to answer the question.
- The game continues until all of the review questions are asked.

PROCEDURE

- Let students know that they will be playing a review game.
- Remind them that when they play games, they have to follow set rules.
- Share your chart with the rules for the review game.
- Play the review game.
- Conclude your review game by reviewing the questions that students answered incorrectly.

MODIFICATIONS: If you have students who need extra help with understanding the rules, provide visual representations of the rules to help them learn and remember the process.

TIPS: Have enough questions prepared so you can allow a chance for every student to answer a review question. You can ask the same question in different ways to accomplish this.

ANCHOR STANDARD ADDRESSED

CCSS.ELA-LITERACY.CCRA.SL.I — Prepare for and participate effectively in a range of conversations and collaborations with diverse partners, building on others' ideas and expressing their own clearly and persuasively.

12. Treasure Hunt

MATERIALS NEEDED

- Student copies of Treasure Map
- Star (one for each child)
- Puzzle piece (one for each child)
- Smiley face sticker (one for each child)
- Index card with the word "rules" written on it (one for each child)

RATIONALE: Creating an environment that is fun and engaging is important in the special needs classroom. The Treasure Hunt activity is a wonderful way to kick off learning and fun in a creative way.

PROCEDURE

o Hide the items for your treasure hunt throughout the classroom.

o Tell students that they will be going on a Treasure Hunt in the classroom.

o Ask students if they have ever gone on a Treasure Hunt before.

- Let students know that this Treasure Hunt will be special because they will be finding things to help make the morning meeting more fun.

- Tell students that they will use the map to find objects in the room. Tell them that the objects are there to be found by each class member.

- Pass out the Treasure Map.

- Let students go on the Treasure Hunt.

- Assist students as necessary to find the objects.

- Once each student has found all four objects, bring them back to the carpet.

- Go over the significance of each object. (Star, because we are all important members of the class; puzzle piece, because we all work together to make the classroom strong; smiley face sticker, because we have fun together during morning meeting; and card that says rules, because we follow the rules during morning meeting so we have a safe and fun meeting.)

MODIFICATIONS: Assist students who will need extra help finding the objects.

Use alternate objects if any of the suggested objects will cause a choking threat.

TIPS: Ensure that your map is easy to read for kids. You can have a child from another classroom come and practice finding the items in the room to see if you need to make any adjustments. Make sure that you have enough items for each student. It is important that each child has the four items in their hand as you go over their significance with the group.

ANCHOR STANDARD ADDRESSED

CCSS.ELA-LITERACY.CCRA.SL.I — Prepare for and participate effectively in a range of conversations and collaborations with diverse partners, building on others' ideas and expressing their own clearly and persuasively.

13. Skits and Drama

MATERIALS NEEDED

- Reader's theater script
- Costumes (optional)
- Video camera or smart phone with recording capability
- Computer
- Projector

RATIONALE: Plays and skits offer a great opportunity to hit on several IEP goals, including communication goals and speaking and listening goals. They also provide a great platform to teach social skills and character education lessons. I have seen teachers use skits and plays to teach numerous social skills in a fun and playful manner.

PREP

o The Internet is full of skits and plays related to social skills. You can find one online or write your own.

o Choose a topic that will best meet the needs of your students. Possible topics include getting along with others, taking turns talking, sharing, etc.

PROCEDURE

o Tell students that they will be performing a skit/play that is related to a special topic.

o If you are writing your own play, you can use language that relates directly to your particular classroom goals.

o Assign students parts and have them practice their lines.

o Have students perform their play/skit, and record it.

o Play the finished skit/play and allow students to enjoy their work.

MODIFICATIONS: If students need help with reading or memorizing their lines, provide extra support.

TIPS: Skits and plays require a lot of patience and time. Be sure to modify your skit/play as necessary. Keep it light and have kids enjoy the process.

ANCHOR STANDARDS ADDRESSED

CCSS.ELA-LITERACY.CCRA.SL.1 — Prepare for and participate effectively in a range of conversations and collaborations with diverse partners, building on others' ideas and expressing their own clearly and persuasively.

CCSS.ELA-LITERACY.CCRA.SL.6 — Adapt speech to a variety of contexts and communicative tasks, demonstrating command of formal English when indicated or appropriate.

14. Using Music

MATERIALS NEEDED

- Music that relates to social skills you want to reinforce
- Chart paper
- Markers

RATIONALE: The connection between music and learning has long been studied. Students with special needs in particular are often stimulated by music to learn. It can be a very motivating factor in your classroom.

PROCEDURE

o Choose a welcome song that your kids will find engaging. There are many children's CDs with welcome songs on them. A few of my favorites are by Raffi, Dr. Jean, and Kidsongs.

o Start the day with your chosen welcome song. You can go around the circle and greet kids as you all sing the songs.

o Consider having a chart stand with the song lyrics written out. This can allow kids to point to the words as you sing to promote one-to-one correspondence.

o As you segue from one song to the other, be sure to cue students in on the next song that you are going to sing. This will allow them to readjust and prepare to join in.

o If you have students who are shy and not participating, go around and sing with them to encourage their participation.

MODIFICATIONS: Some students may not like music and find it unsettling. Always have the option for kids to sit out during music time.

If you have students with hearing impairment, be sure to have alternative ways for them to enjoy the music.

Some students may need to listen with headphones. Have them readily available if necessary.

TIPS: When choosing music to play during your morning meeting, it is important to know your students likes and needs. Some children are more accustomed to soft music while others are set off by loud music. It will be important to know these preferences so you can choose music that will fit the tastes of all your learners. You can make music more interactive by asking kids to pick the songs that will be played for the day. This helps to build their self-esteem and gives them an opportunity to be active participants in their learning.

ANCHOR STANDARDS ADDRESSED

CCSS.ELA-LITERACY.CCRA.SL.I — Prepare for and participate effectively in a range of conversations and collaborations with diverse partners, building on others' ideas and expressing their own clearly and persuasively.

15. Brain Breaks

MATERIALS NEEDED

- Videos with wiggle activities. There are many free websites that offer brain break activities. Many of the websites teach dance moves that are fun and engaging.

RATIONALE: Students often need to wiggle and decompress when they have to sit for extended times. Brains breaks are a great tool to use to accomplish this.

PROCEDURE

o When kids have been sitting for too long and start to get wiggly, let them know you are going to have a brain break.

o Have the kids get up and get their wiggles out.

o Watch a few of the videos and make up some moves of your own.

o Kids will soon begin to let you know when they need a brain break.

MODIFICATIONS: If you have students who need extra help in getting their wiggles out, be sure to have staff available to assist.

TIPS: Brain break time must be structured and monitored. Ensure that you teach the appropriate behavior for the brain break time. Don't be afraid to practice the brain break routine.

ANCHOR STANDARD ADDRESSED

CCSS.ELA-LITERACY.CCRA.SL.1 — Prepare for and participate effectively in a range of conversations and collaborations with diverse partners, building on others' ideas and expressing their own clearly and persuasively.

16. Classroom Community Artifacts

MATERIALS NEEDED
- Table to display artifacts
- Labels
- Artifacts

RATIONALE: Your morning meeting area needs to be inclusive. One way to accomplish this is to display artifacts related to the time and activities your class has produced during morning meeting. This is a wonderful way to display student artifacts to support self-esteem.

PROCEDURE
- Let students know that you will be setting up a classroom gallery to showcase all the wonderful things you have done together during morning meeting.
- Ask students if they know what a gallery is.
- Talk about the fact that treasures that we cherish are kept in a museum.
- Let them know that the time you spend in morning meeting is a treasure and that you cherish all the time you spend together.
- Let them know that one way you want to capture all the fun and learning that occurs during morning meeting is to display some of their best work in the morning meeting gallery so they can admire it throughout the day during their free time.
- Use labels like in a museum to explain the works on display.
- Have a few pieces ready to start the display.

MODIFICATIONS: Ensure that students have assistance with completing projects so they can have something to display.

TIPS: Update your gallery displays monthly. You can set a time at the beginning of the month during morning meeting to showcase the new items in the gallery. Make sure that each child has something on display each month.

CCSS.ELA-LITERACY.CCRA.SL.I — Prepare for and participate effectively in a range of conversations and collaborations with diverse partners, building on others' ideas and expressing their own clearly and persuasively.

CCSS.ELA-LITERACY.CCRA.SL.5 — Make strategic use of digital media and visual displays of data to express information and enhance understanding of presentations.

17. Lesson on Community

MATERIALS NEEDED

- Picture of the community
- Chart paper
- Markers
- Children's book about a community that works together
- Sticky notes

RATIONALE: It is important to make connections to the outside world when you teach. Morning meeting is all about building community. One way to hit this home is to teach a lesson on community and talk about the similarities in the classroom community.

PROCEDURE

o Tell students that they will be learning about community today.

o Ask students what they think the word "community" means.

o Display a picture of the community so kids can use this as a tool to come up with their responses.

o Using the marker, record their responses on chart paper.

o Share the definition of community with the class. Write the following on a chart: "Community: a group of people working together for the common good."

o Tell students your classroom is a community that works together for the good of the class.

o Tell students that you will be reading a story about community.

o Tell students that they will have a job as you are reading. Their job is to think about how your classroom community is like the community in the story.

o Write the words "Our Classroom Community" on a new piece of chart paper. Let students know that when they find similarities between the characters in the story and your class, you will record them on the chart.

o Read the story to the class. As you are reading, stop at points where the characters are sharing or working in groups. Ask how the people in the story are doing things similar to how your class works together.

o At the conclusion of the story, go back over the similarities that were found.

o Have students share what they learned about community from the book and how it relates to the classroom community.

MODIFICATIONS: If students need more prompting to find the connections, be sure to provide this scaffold.

Ensure the book that you share has characters that you students can relate to.

TIPS: In order for this activity to be successful, read the story ahead of time and mark it with sticky notes with question prompts. This will ensure you hone in on the community connections you want to reinforce.

ANCHOR STANDARD ADDRESSED

CCSS.ELA-LITERACY.CCRA.SL.I — Prepare for and participate effectively in a range of conversations and collaborations with diverse partners, building on others' ideas and expressing their own clearly and persuasively.

18. Community Project

MATERIALS NEEDED
- Online video about a community project
- Computer or laptop
- Projector

RATIONALE: Having students work on a community project is a wonderful way to broaden their understanding of the importance of helping others. This important social skill enables students to have more empathy for each other.

PROCEDURE
o Tell students that you have an exciting opportunity for them: they will be working on a community project to help make the neighborhood better.

o Share an online video about a group of students working on a community project.

o After the video, ask students what they learned from the video.

o Have students share their ideas.

o Share the community project that your class will take part in.

o Explain all the details regarding what the project will entail.

o Assign students different jobs to help accomplish your goal.

MODIFICATIONS: Assign jobs that relate to your students' strengths. If a student needs assistance, be sure to have a plan in place to accomplish this.

TIPS: There are so many community projects that your class can get involved in. Our school has a community garden. You can look at a recycling program or a program to clean the playground. Base your community project on your community needs. Take the time to research different projects that are available in your city. You will be surprised by the opportunities for partnership that exist.

CCSS.ELA-LITERACY.CCRA.SL.I — Prepare for and participate effectively in a range of conversations and collaborations with diverse partners, building on others' ideas and expressing their own clearly and persuasively.

19. Bringing in Community Members

MATERIALS NEEDED
- A community member
- Chart paper
- Markers

RATIONALE: Brining in community helpers to explain their jobs is a wonderful way to allow your students to connect with their world. Students often have great respect for community members and find it an honor to have them come in and speak with them.

PROCEDURE
- Let students know that a very special community member is going to speak with them about their job.

- Let them know their job is to listen and think about questions they want to ask the community member at the end of their presentation.

- Have your community member speak to the class.

- After the community member speaks, allow the children to ask questions.

- After the community member leaves, talk with your class about the importance of having community members to help make our world better.

- Draw the connection to the class and how important they are in making the classroom community better.

- Have the class write a thank you letter with the markers on chart paper to send to the community member. Have all the classmates sign the letter.

MODIFICATIONS: Have assistance readily available for students who may need help in articulating their questions.

☛ **TIPS:** Have a meeting before your community member arrives and let them know the key points you want them to go over with your class. Some possible community helpers to invite are police officers, firefighters, nurses, bankers, etc.

CCSS.ELA-LITERACY.CCRA.SL.I — Prepare for and participate effectively in a range of conversations and collaborations with diverse partners, building on others' ideas and expressing their own clearly and persuasively.

CCSS.ELA-LITERACY.CCRA.W.4 — Produce clear and coherent writing in which the development, organization, and style are appropriate to task, purpose, and audience.

Chapter 3
STRATEGIES FOR SOCIAL DEVELOPMENT

Numerous research studies have indicated that when students feel safe and secure, their academic achievement increases. One way to help build this sense of security is to foster an environment that is welcoming and inclusive. A morning meeting focused on building social and emotional intelligence builds such an environment. Collaboration and comradery flow naturally within the morning meeting framework.

This chapter highlights strategies to help your students build their social and emotional development. Some of the key strategies reinforced are listening, taking turns, and disagreeing appropriately. The 20 strategies shared here can be easily implemented and tweaked to meet the individual needs of your classroom.

20. Morning Check-In

MATERIALS NEEDED

- Morning Check-In chart

RATIONALE: Following routines like a morning check is a wonderful way to ensure students have a stress-free morning transition. Routines help students feel safe, which increases their ability to learn.

PREP

Prepare a Morning Check-In chart. It can include the following: Hang up your backpack, put your folder away, sign in, sharpen your pencil, take a seat at the morning meeting spot, etc. Modify your chart accordingly.

PROCEDURE

- Introduce your Morning Check-In chart.

- Go over each item on the chart explicitly.

- Have children ask any questions they have regarding any item on the chart.

- Let students know that each day they come in, they will independently complete each item on the chart.

- For the first week, model each item one by one and watch students as they complete the task.

- As students become more familiar with the routine you can take away the scaffold.

MODIFICATIONS: Add pictures to the Morning Check-In chart to support students.

TIPS: Continue to practice the routine until students master them. Time taken to practice to perfection is well spent.

CCSS.ELA-LITERACY.CCRA.SL.I — Prepare for and participate effectively in a range of conversations and collaborations with diverse partners, building on others' ideas and expressing their own clearly and persuasively.

21. Listening

MATERIALS NEEDED

- Picture of an ear
- Chart paper
- Markers

RATIONALE: Listening and following directions is often implied in IEP goals. The skill of listening can be related to speech goals, behavioral goals, and several other areas. This activity will address any of the areas the goal is incorporated in.

PROCEDURE

- Put a picture of an ear on the board. Ask students why they think the ear is important.

- Have students share their ideas. Take any and all contributions.

- Tell students that the reason our ears are important is for listening.

- Tell them that listening is one of the most important skills we need in order to learn in school.

- Talk to kids about the fire alarm and the daily announcements. Tell them that both are important because they signify important information or a warning.

o Let them know that just as it is important to listen to announcements to follow procedure and listen to the fire alarm, it is important to listen during morning meeting.

o Tell students that one of your rules is to listen with their eyes on the speaker and their mouths closed to show that they are listening.

o Have students practice listening to one another speak.

o Model this activity first with another student.

o Be very explicit about having eye contact and not speaking, but listening when the other person talks.

o After the students have taken turns listening to one another, have them come back to attention.

o Ask them to share how they felt when the other person was listening to them.

o Write their responses on the chart.

o Finish the activity by reminding students about the importance of listening and what listening looks and sounds like.

MODIFICATIONS: If students need more time practicing listening, be sure to include this lesson multiple times.

☛ **TIPS:** Talk about activities that are important to your kids in regard to listening. We have monthly fire drills and morning announcements at our school. You may have other times when students need to actively listen. Taking the time to practice the morning meeting routine to get out the kinks will be necessary as you continue to build this structure into your classroom. You will need to tweak specific parts of the routine in order to change behavior and progress.

ANCHOR STANDARD ADDRESSED

CCSS.ELA-LITERACY.CCRA.SL.I — Prepare for and participate effectively in a range of conversations and collaborations with diverse partners, building on others' ideas and expressing their own clearly and persuasively.

22. Asking and Answering Questions

RATIONALE: Asking and answering questions is an important skill for students to master. It is a part of IEP goals for speech and behavior and Common Core ELA standards, and it can easily be incorporated in any activity that you present.

PROCEDURE

o After morning meeting has become a part of your routine, pick a day to practice some of the areas of the routine that need to be perfected.

o Use professional sports players who practice to get better at what they do as an analogy for practicing the morning routine to get better at it.

o Let students know that you will practice some of the steps of the morning routine that need to be improved.

o Be overly explicit and dramatic when you practice the necessary steps of the morning meeting that need tweaking.

o Once you have practiced, ask the kids to rate their performance. The questions you ask students to answer about the practice should be prepared ahead of time to allow a smooth flow.

o Let students know that you will continue to practice as necessary until they have the steps down to perfection.

MODIFICATIONS: There may only be individual students who need to practice particular parts of the morning routine. If this is the case, set aside time to work with kids individually.

☛ **TIPS:** Be sure to maintain a positive and upbeat demeanor as you practice the skills. You want to ensure that students see the importance of practicing, but don't feel deflated or overly criticized.

ANCHOR STANDARDS ADDRESSED

CCSS.ELA-LITERACY.CCRA.SL.1 — Prepare for and participate effectively in a range of conversations and collaborations with diverse partners, building on others' ideas and expressing their own clearly and persuasively.

CCSS.ELA-LITERACY.CCRA.SL.6 — Adapt speech to a variety of contexts and communicative tasks, demonstrating command of formal English when indicated or appropriate.

23. Rate Your Day

MATERIALS NEEDED

- Markers
- Student copies of Rate My Day sheet (page 240)

RATIONALE: Having the ability to self-monitor one's behavior is an important life skill. This activity will provide students with a tool to use in learning to self-manage and rate their behavior.

PROCEDURE

- Let students know that you will be sharing a rating sheet that they can use to rate their behavior throughout the day.
- Start by rating the whole group's behavior during morning meeting.
- Each day for at least a week, fill out the rating sheet for the class.
- Have the students help you fill out the rating sheet.
- On the following week, have the students rate their own behavior during morning meeting.
- Continue to scaffold and support as needed so kids can internalize the process.

MODIFICATIONS: Provide added support for students who need extra help rating their behavior. Ensure that kids understand the criteria for the rating. If the child is unaware of how they are feeling, provide those extra supports until they are able to internalize the learning.

CCSS.ELA-LITERACY.CCRA.SL.1 — Prepare for and participate effectively in a range of conversations and collaborations with diverse partners, building on others' ideas and expressing their own clearly and persuasively.

24. Sharing Examples

MATERIALS NEEDED

- Anchor charts, videos, or skits
- Chart paper
- Marker

RATIONALE: The morning meeting provides a perfect opportunity to share examples for academic and behavioral goals. This time of community is non-threatening and students are apt to take on new learning quickly.

PROCEDURE

o Create a routine for sharing examples during your morning meeting.

o Your routine may include using anchor charts, video examples, or skits to share the desired learning.

o When creating examples, think about the dominant learning style of your students.

o Take the most popular learning style and ensure you provide examples using that learning mode.

o The modeling procedure will include an introduction to the behavior or skill being modeled.

o Ask students to discuss what they see, hear, or learned after the model.

o Capture those ideas on a chart.

MODIFICATIONS: Modify the examples that you share with your students depending on their learning style and areas of need.

🏴 **TIPS:** Be sure that you provide examples that work and don't work. For instance, if you are demonstrating what you want in a project, provide samples that show an acceptable project and one that is not acceptable.

ANCHOR STANDARD ADDRESSED

CCSS.ELA-LITERACY.CCRA.SL.I — Prepare for and participate effectively in a range of conversations and collaborations with diverse partners, building on others' ideas and expressing their own clearly and persuasively.

25. Eye Contact

MATERIALS NEEDED
- Chart paper
- Markers

RATIONALE: Being able to maintain appropriate eye contact when speaking to others is an important social skill. You can easily reinforce this skill during morning meeting sharing time and other times when kids are listening to a speaker.

PROCEDURE
- Let students know that they are going to be practicing how to maintain proper eye contact when speaking to someone.
- Ask kids why they think having good eye contact is important.
- Use the markers to write down the ideas students share on chart paper.
- After soliciting their ideas, share with students that maintaining eye contact helps the speaker know you are listening and allows the listener to really understand what the other person is saying.
- Call on volunteers to model using appropriate eye contact.
- Give students a prompt to use when they practice. Prompts may include what they had for breakfast or what they want to be when they grow up.
- Write the following on the chart: "Eye contact means looking the speaker in the eye and listening with your ears open and mouth closed."
- You may also draw a picture to represent what eye contact looks like.
- Practice proper eye contact with your volunteer(s).
- After each practice, have the kids share what they noticed during the practice.
- Pair students and have them practice giving eye contact to a speaker.
- Monitor and provide immediate feedback to the students.

- After each student has had a chance to model eye contact, have them share their experience with the eye contact activity.

- Remind students that eye contact is important and that you will continue practicing it during morning meeting.

MODIFICATIONS: Some students may need support with maintaining eye contact. You can practice this with the student in a smaller setting or one on one.

ANCHOR STANDARDS ADDRESSED

CCSS.ELA-LITERACY.CCRA.SL.1 — Prepare for and participate effectively in a range of conversations and collaborations with diverse partners, building on others' ideas and expressing their own clearly and persuasively.

CCSS.ELA-LITERACY.CCRA.SL.3 — Evaluate a speaker's point of view, reasoning, and use of evidence and rhetoric.

26. Body Language

MATERIALS NEEDED

- Chart paper
- Markers

RATIONALE: Understanding the implications of body language is an important skill to teach to students. We often overlook its importance. This is a social cuing skill that will help students in the classroom and beyond.

PROCEDURE

o Let students know that you will be talking about body language and its importance in their daily life.

o Ask students how they greet someone who tells them hello.

o Have students share their responses.

o Record their responses on the chart paper.

o Talk about how you can shake hands, raise your hand to say hi, or high five to say hello depending on who are greeting.

o Tell students that they will be practicing saying hello and goodbye today using appropriate body language.

o Divide students into groups of two or three.

o Have them model saying hello and goodbye.

o Monitor students as they work on the activity, and provide feedback.

o At the conclusion of the lesson, pull students together and talk about the different ways they use their bodies to say hello and goodbye.

o Have some kids share how they practiced saying hello and goodbye with their partner.

o Tell students you will continue to practice appropriate body language in class.

TIPS: Be sure to pair students up with classmates that they will have success working with. Think about their personalities and abilities when pairing students.

CCSS.ELA-LITERACY.CCRA.SL.I — Prepare for and participate effectively in a range of conversations and collaborations with diverse partners, building on others' ideas and expressing their own clearly and persuasively.

27. Respect

MATERIALS NEEDED

- Chart paper with word "RESPECT" written horizontally
- Markers

RATIONALE: Teaching students the importance of respect is crucial to ensure they model the appropriate respectful behavior and language expected in the classroom. This activity serves as a fun way to reinforce this skill.

PROCEDURE

o Tell students that they will be learning about respect.

o Ask students if they know what the word "respect" means.

o Take any and all responses.

o Show students your chart with the word "respect" written on it.

o Tell them you are going to learn about what the word respect means by looking at each letter in the word.

o Start with the letter R. Write the word "responsible" vertically beneath the letter R. Tell kids that when you show respect, you have responsible behavior. This means you are always helpful and kind to others.

o Write the letter E. Write the word "equal" vertically beneath the letter E. Tell kids that when you show respect, you know that everyone is equal and you treat everyone with the same respect.

o Write the letter S. Write the word "sympathy" vertically beneath the letter S. Tell kids that when you show respect, you have sympathy for others. This means you care about others and their feelings.

o Write the letter P. Write the word "positive" vertically beneath the letter P. Tell kids that when you show respect, you show positive behavior. This means you do not put others down but find positives in everyone.

o Write the letter E. Write the word "explain" vertically beneath the letter E. Tell kids that when you show respect, you give everyone the chance to explain how they are feeling. This means you listen to others and let them explain themselves.

- o Write the letter C. Write the word "caring" vertically beneath the letter C. Tell kids that when you show respect, you have a caring heart. This means you care about your teammates and how they are doing.

- o Write the letter T. Write the word "together" vertically beneath the letter T. Tell kids that when you show respect, you work well together with others. This means you share and work with others in your group.

- o Post the completed chart in a prominent place. Tell students that when you see them showing any of the behaviors that represent respect, you will acknowledge their efforts.

☛ **TIPS:** Go overboard with acknowledging respectful behavior with your kids. This will help instill the traits of respect and allow students to recognize it in action.

ANCHOR STANDARD ADDRESSED

CCSS.ELA-LITERACY.CCRA.SL.I — Prepare for and participate effectively in a range of conversations and collaborations with diverse partners, building on others' ideas and expressing their own clearly and persuasively.

28. Character Traits

MATERIALS NEEDED

- Chart paper with list of character traits you want to focus on
- Markers

RATIONALE: Character traits are the pillars of life. Teaching them is pivotal to the internalization of the skills. Character training has been around for several decades. Having a focused time like morning meeting to use a platform for teaching the skills is an effective strategy to reinforce the skills.

PREP

o On a piece of chart paper, write a list of character traits that you want to focus on with your students. Be creative with your chart and use different colors and shapes to write the words.

PROCEDURE

o Show the chart to your students. Ask them what they know about any of the words listed on the chart.

o Take any and all responses.

o Go over the list of character traits listed on your chart by reading each word and giving a child-friendly definition for the word.

o Pick one word to focus on for the week.

o Write the focus word and frame it so it has prominence in the room.

o Take the time to teach on the importance of the focus character trait and let students know you will be modeling it each day during morning meeting.

o Each day, talk about the focus word and share examples of the trait in storybooks or other sources.

MODIFICATIONS: Provide individual time to teach each character trait to students who need more individualized attention.

TIPS: Do your homework and find books and other sources on your new character trait well before morning meeting. This way you can read the story beforehand and have examples you want to share.

ANCHOR STANDARDS ADDRESSED

CCSS.ELA-LITERACY.CCRA.R.3 — Analyze how and why individuals, events, and ideas develop and interact over the course of a text.

CCSS.ELA-LITERACY.CCRA.SL.I — Prepare for and participate effectively in a range of conversations and collaborations with diverse partners, building on others' ideas and expressing their own clearly and persuasively.

29. Building Character

MATERIALS NEEDED

- Markers
- Large cube pattern
- Template to build cubes

RATIONALE: Using an art project to reinforce character traits is a great way to assess student understanding and provide an engaging activity.

PROCEDURE

o Teach the Character Traits lesson (page 72).

o Review the character traits you have covered with your class.

o This review can include a discussion on each trait and an explanation/ example from students.

o Let students know that they are going to be making cubes to play a game in relation to character traits.

o Have a larger cube pattern ready so you can model for your students.

o Pick a character trait to illustrate on your cube.

o On one side, write the name of the trait.

o On the other side, write a definition.

o On a third side, draw an illustration to depict the trait.

o On the remaining three sides of the cube, draw pictures that depict the trait.

o Assemble your cube once you have completed these tasks.

o Let students know they will follow the same process you modeled to define and illustrate a cube of their own.

o Have each student pick a character trait they would like to illustrate.

o To ensure that everyone does not illustrate the same trait, give students a choice between two or three traits to illustrate.

o Give students time to work on their project and assemble it.

- Once all the cubes are assembled, have students turn in their cubes.

- Put the cubes in a box with a hole so that you can shake the cubes and have one come out.

- Once the cube comes out, have the kids model the character trait in action or by using words.

- Continue to shake the box until all cubes have been used.

MODIFICATIONS: Some students may need to refer back to the chart as they complete their work. In a prominent place in the room display the character traits chart so kids can easily refer back to it.

TIPS: Have assistance available for kids who need help with illustrating or assembling their cubes.

ANCHOR STANDARDS ADDRESSED

CCSS.ELA-LITERACY.CCRA.SL.I — Prepare for and participate effectively in a range of conversations and collaborations with diverse partners, building on others' ideas and expressing their own clearly and persuasively.

CCSS.ELA-LITERACY.CCRA.W.4 — Produce clear and coherent writing in which the development, organization, and style are appropriate to task, purpose, and audience.

30. Character Map

MATERIALS NEEDED
- Get to Know Your Character template (page 241)
- Chart paper
- Markers
- Example

RATIONALE: Character mapping is an excellent tool to allow students to express their understanding of different character traits. It is a fun, nonthreatening activity that can be used with any character being studied.

PROCEDURE
- After you have spent a few weeks talking about character traits, introduce the Get to Know Your Character template.
- Let students know that they will be filling in a Get to Know Your Character template as a whole group.
- Copy the format for the Get to Know Your Character template on a piece of chart paper.
- Choose a character to explore.
- Fill out the different parts on the Get to Know Your Character template with the class.
- Elicit responses from all students to get total participation.
- Once you have filled out your sample template, let the students know that they will be filling out a template of their own.
- Have a predetermined character for kids to write/draw about in their character map.
- Release students to work on their maps.
- Bring students back together and have them share their maps.

MODIFICATIONS: Modify the number of responses students will answer on their Get to Know Your Character templates as necessary. Have supports in place for kids who may need assistance with completion.

ANCHOR STANDARDS ADDRESSED

CCSS.ELA-LITERACY.CCRA.SL.I — Prepare for and participate effectively in a range of conversations and collaborations with diverse partners, building on others' ideas and expressing their own clearly and persuasively.

CCSS.ELA-LITERACY.CCRA.W.4 — Produce clear and coherent writing in which the development, organization, and style are appropriate to task, purpose, and audience.

31. Character Web

MATERIALS NEEDED
- Chart paper
- Markers
- Character Web template (page 242)

RATIONALE: Allowing students to use graphic organizers to structure their thoughts is a wonderful strategy to promote thinking. The Character Web provides a great opportunity to brainstorm and share ideas.

PROCEDURE
- Once you have taught students activity #29, Building Character (page 74), create a classroom Character Web to explore different character traits.

- Tell students that they will be creating a Character Web.

- Explain that a Character Web is used to capture different traits of a character.

- Go through the process of filling out the Character Web.

- Have students share traits they see in the character and add them to the web.

- Once the Web is complete, have students share what they enjoyed about the activity.

MODIFICATIONS: Provide additional think time for students that need more time to come up with ideas for the Web.

CCSS.ELA-LITERACY.CCRA.SL.I — Prepare for and participate effectively in a range of conversations and collaborations with diverse partners, building on others' ideas and expressing their own clearly and persuasively.

CCSS.ELA-LITERACY.CCRA.W.4 — Produce clear and coherent writing in which the development, organization, and style are appropriate to task, purpose, and audience.

32. What Would You Do?

MATERIALS NEEDED

- Chart paper
- Markers
- Strips of paper with role-playing situations written on them.

RATIONALE: Practicing how they would respond to particular situations is a great exercise to prepare students for the real world. This activity allows them to simulate circumstances through role-play.

PREP

- Prepare strips of paper with various role-playing situations written on them. Examples can include what to do if someone were to ask how to get to the main office, or how to find the nurse's office.

PROCEDURE

- Tell students that they are going engage in a role-playing game called "What Would You Do?"

- Ask students if they have ever participated in a play or did any role-playing.

- Let students know that they will be practicing social skills by role-playing situations.

- Tell students that you will start by demonstrating what role-playing means.

- Tell students that you are going to pretend that someone has asked you for help on an assignment.

- Have a class volunteer play the role of the person needing help.

- Role-play the scenario with your volunteer.

- Ask students what they noticed during your role-play.

- Write the words "What Would You Do?" at the top of a piece of chart paper and record student responses.

- Mention that you were helpful and friendly in order to highlight this behavior.

- Pass out your strips of paper with other role-playing situations.

- Have students pair up and take one scenario to role-play.

- Release students to practice their role-playing. Let them know they will switch roles in two minutes.

- Have the students switch roles and complete the activity again.

- Bring students back together.

- Have volunteers share their role-playing in front of the class.

MODIFICATIONS: Provide alternative activities to role-play depending on the students' needs.

ANCHOR STANDARDS ADDRESSED

CCSS.ELA-LITERACY.CCRA.SL.1 — Prepare for and participate effectively in a range of conversations and collaborations with diverse partners, building on others' ideas and expressing their own clearly and persuasively.

CCSS.ELA-LITERACY.CCRA.SL.2 — Integrate and evaluate information presented in diverse media and formats, including visually, quantitatively, and orally.

33. Complimenting Others

MATERIALS NEEDED

- Chart paper
- Markers
- Bulletin board
- Decorated cards for each student

RATIONALE: Learning how to give and receive compliments is an important life skill. Often students with special needs require more explicit teaching on how to give and receive compliments. This activity is a perfect channel for teaching this skill.

PROCEDURE

- Write the word "compliment" on a piece of chart paper.
- Ask students to share definitions and examples of compliments.

- Reveal your bulletin board.

- Explain to students that this board will be used to post compliments for the class.

- Let them know you will add compliments and that they will also be responsible for adding compliments.

- Give each student a decorated card.

- Ask them to write one compliment for a classmate on it.

- Give kids time to write their compliment.

- Have students share their cards and post them on the compliment board.

- Use the compliment board whenever you find a need to build community and celebrate.

MODIFICATIONS: Provide assistance for students that need help with writing their compliment cards.

TIPS: Keep the compliment board alive by visiting it periodically. You don't want the board to become stagnant. To avoid this, create a routine, possibly weekly, to add to the compliment board.

ANCHOR STANDARDS ADDRESSED

CCSS.ELA-LITERACY.CCRA.SL.1 — Prepare for and participate effectively in a range of conversations and collaborations with diverse partners, building on others' ideas and expressing their own clearly and persuasively.

CCSS.ELA-LITERACY.CCRA.W.4 — Produce clear and coherent writing in which the development, organization, and style are appropriate to task, purpose, and audience.

34. Problem-Solving Activity

MATERIALS NEEDED

- Chart paper
- Markers
- Numerous age appropriate puzzles for groups of two to three students.

RATIONALE: Working in teams to solve problems is an important skill to foster. The following activity can help reinforce team building and problem solving.

PROCEDURE

- Let students know that they will be solving a problem together as a group.
- Explain that it is easier to solve problems when you do it as a team.

o Ask students if they have ever had to solve a problem.

o Take any and all student contributions.

o Put students into groups of two.

o Give each group the task of completing a puzzle.

o Tell them that they have to work together as a team to complete the puzzle.

o Set the timer for two minutes.

o Walk around and make notes regarding how the teams are working together to solve the puzzle.

o Once the times goes off bring the team back together.

o Discuss how it felt to work in a team to complete the puzzle.

o Record student responses on the board.

o End the activity by reiterating how much quicker it is when you work together in teams to solve problems.

o Explain that just as it was quicker to complete the puzzle as a team, in life, it is better to solve problems when you work together.

o Explain that your classroom community is a team that works together to solve problems.

MODIFICATIONS: Group students according to ability to complete the activity. Some students may need support when working in the group activity. Have plans for assistance readily available.

🏴 **TIPS:** Choose puzzles that will be a challenge for the team members. Do not choose puzzles that the kids can solve alone. You can borrow puzzles from other teachers or colleagues to use for this activity.

CCSS.ELA-LITERACY.CCRA.SL.1 — Prepare for and participate effectively in a range of conversations and collaborations with diverse partners, building on others' ideas and expressing their own clearly and persuasively.

35. Communication Circle

MATERIALS NEEDED

- Picture cards with individuals, animals, etc., that need something. For example, a dirty car that needs to be washed or a child that fell and needs a Band-Aid.

RATIONALE: Communication goals are often found in student IEPs. This activity helps students practice communicating effectively to express needs and wants. Effective communication is a necessary life skill that students need to be explicitly taught. This activity teaches communication in a playful manner that is very effective.

PROCEDURE

o Write the word communication on the board.

o Tell students that they will be playing a game today to show how to communicate or share their ideas.

o Ask students if they have ever heard the word "communication."

o Have students share what they know about the word "communication."

o Write the following definition on the board following the word "communication:" sending and receiving information.

o Tell students that they are going to play a game where they have to share with the class what their partner shares with them.

o Tell them that they have to listen carefully to make sure that they share the correct information.

o Pair students and give each pair a picture card.

o Have students use the following sentence frame to discuss the needs being communicated in the pictures: "The ____ in my picture needs _____."

o Have students go around and share what their partner shared with them regarding their picture.

o After the activity, have students share what they liked about the activity and what they found challenging.

o End by reiterating how important listening is in communication. We have to ensure we listen closely so we can share the correct information.

MODIFICATIONS: Modify or make changes in the picture given, according to student need. Practice with students who may need extra help before they share. Some students may need help with the vocabulary to share what the person or thing in their picture needs. Be readily available to provide this support.

36. Reporting Out

MATERIALS NEEDED
- Chart paper
- Colorful markers

RATIONALE: Assessment is a huge part of the teaching and learning cycle. Teaching students to report their learning is important to assess how much they've absorbed. One simple way to assess student learning is to have them share what they've learned using a clear and concise method. This activity can be used for any subject. The morning routine is an excellent way to introduce it.

PROCEDURE

- At the conclusion of your morning meeting, let students know you are going to share a simple way that you will be checking on their learning.
- Explain that it is important to touch base on what they have learned before moving on to something new.
- Write the following on the chart paper:
- 2 things I learned (draw boxes to fill in)
- 1 question I have (draw a box to fill in)
- Make the activity game-like by using colorful markers and graphics to fill in the boxes.
- Work collaboratively with students to fill out the boxes.
- Let students know that you will use this process to assess their learning after teaching.

MODIFICATIONS: Provide extra scaffolding for students who need help filling out the chart.

🐾 **TIPS:** To make this activity game-like, you can do it as a review game. Students can be called on to share what they learned and you can make it like a jeopardy game where kids have to answer in question format what they learned. There is really no limit to the ways you can present this activity to make it more fun.

CCSS.ELA-LITERACY.CCRA.SL.I — Prepare for and participate effectively in a range of conversations and collaborations with diverse partners, building on others' ideas and expressing their own clearly and persuasively.

37. Emotion Bingo

MATERIALS NEEDED
- Chart paper
- Emotion bingo game cards
- Chips or markers to fill in the spaces
- Scenario cards

RATIONALE: It's important for students to understand that we all experience different emotions. This bingo games provides an opportunity to see different scenarios and the emotions they evoke.

PREP
o Create an emotion bingo play board. Simply place emoticons that illustrate different behaviors that will be included on your scenario cards. You can find different faces for your bingo cards online. There are many free images you can download. Use stock paper, if you have it, so your cards are more durable.

o Create scenario cards that describe each emotion on your bingo card. For example: Sam lost her watch. How is she feeling? Answer: sad.

PROCEDURE
o Tell students that they will be playing a game today related to how they feel.

o Explain that emotions are strong feelings we can experience.

o Share a personal example of when you have felt happy.

o Have student volunteers share their examples.

o Introduce the emotion bingo game.

o Explain that it is like traditional bingo, but you will be reading different scenarios and students have to figure out which picture to cover based on the scenario.

o Go over the different emotions on the game board. Read the scenario cards and have students share which emotion the card is explaining.

o As students become more familiar with the routine, you will be able to move through the cards more quickly.

o The person to fill their entire board wins.

MODIFICATIONS: If individual students need assistance with covering their cards, provide this scaffold.

ANCHOR STANDARD ADDRESSED

CCSS.ELA-LITERACY.CCRA.SL.I — Prepare for and participate effectively in a range of conversations and collaborations with diverse partners, building on others' ideas and expressing their own clearly and persuasively.

38. How Do I Feel Today?

MATERIALS NEEDED

- Bulletin board titled "How Do I Feel Today?"
- Pockets on the board with each child's name written on them
- Set of cards to place in the pocket with different emotions (happy, sad, excited, scared, angry, etc.)

RATIONALE: One way to teach the IEP goal of exhibiting self-control and emotional constraint is by having kids assess their own emotions. This activity provides a quick check-in at the beginning of the day when students have the opportunity to express themselves and get their day off to a good start.

PROCEDURE

- Draw students' attention to the How Do I Feel Today bulletin board.
- Explain that each day they come in, they will choose a card that expresses how they are feeling.
- Discuss that we all experience different emotions and that it is not uncommon to experience different emotions throughout the day.
- Model how to use the board by calling on a student to share how they feel.
- They will then go over to the board and place the appropriate card in the pocket.
- Have each student place the appropriate card in the pocket corresponding to their name.
- Invite the students to change their emotion cards throughout the day.
- For a week, repeat this activity until students learn to do it independently.

MODIFICATIONS: Provide assistance if students need help determining how they feel. Some students may need more coaching on understanding their feelings. You can accomplish this by talking about feelings and reading the books listed in the Additional Resources chapter.

TIPS: This activity can help students become more in tune with how they are feeling. It can also help you determine what time of day and what transitions or activities cause students stress or emotional swings. Use this information to help decrease such instances.

ANCHOR STANDARD ADDRESSED

CCSS.ELA-LITERACY.CCRA.SL.I — Prepare for and participate effectively in a range of conversations and collaborations with diverse partners, building on others' ideas and expressing their own clearly and persuasively.

39. Taking Turns

MATERIALS NEEDED
- Chart paper
- Markers

RATIONALE: Being able to play in cooperative manner is a common IEP goal for students. This activity is a wonderful way to teach this important skill. The ability to wait one's turn is an important life skill that children will need to master throughout life. Modeling the appropriate behavior during morning meeting is a nonthreatening way to teach this skill.

PROCEDURE
- Let students know that during morning meeting they will often have to take turns to complete tasks.
- Tell students that when they take turns, they enjoy doing things more with others.
- Model taking turns with a student.
- Overexaggerate how much better you work with others when you take turns.
- Have students model taking turns with another classmate.
- Go around and monitor as students take turns.
- Provide feedback as necessary.
- Have students share what they liked about taking turns.
- Write their responses on the board.
- Create a chart with the class on what taking turns looks and sounds like.
- Post the chart in a prominent area to refer to when necessary.

MODIFICATIONS: There may be students that need more practice with taking turns. Set up time to role play and model taking turns with these students to help solidify the learning.

CCSS.ELA-LITERACY.CCRA.SL.I — Prepare for and participate effectively in a range of conversations and collaborations with diverse partners, building on others' ideas and expressing their own clearly and persuasively.

Chapter 4

STRATEGIES FOR SKILLS DEVELOPMENT IN ENGLISH LANGUAGE ARTS AND SOCIAL STUDIES

English language arts and social studies are subjects that blend naturally in the morning meeting routine. Read alouds and group writing fit naturally in the morning meeting routine. What is especially unique about incorporating English language arts and social studies is that these subjects can be used to reinforce social skills, character development, and problem solving.

You can easily find literature that connects with character development. Students learn concepts and build connections when you share strategies or skills by using literature. This chapter offers many suggestions for ways to incorporate literacy and social studies in the morning meeting routine. One caveat to keep in mind is to pick books that are inclusive so you can provide role models for your students.

40. Rhymes and Chants

MATERIALS NEEDED

- Chart paper
- Markers
- Chart with rhyme or chant
- Individual copy of rhyme or chant for each student

RATIONALE: Listening to and reciting rhymes and chants is an easy way to reinforce literacy skills. Rhymes and chants provide phonemic awareness, fluency, and one-to-one correspondence teaching, to name a few benefits. Rhyming not only helps prepare students to read, but also increases their oral language skills.

PREP

Write the words to a rhyme or chant on chart paper.

PROCEDURE

o Pick a rhyme or chant that goes along with a theme or project that you are working on in class.

o Teach students the new rhyme or chant by pointing to the words as you teach them.

o You can call on volunteers to point with you if you desire.

o After reciting the rhyme or chant, have kids practice with a partner so they can easily memorize the new rhyme/chant.

o Extend the activity by having students write rhymes or chants.

o Provide students with a starting point on the rhyme scheme you want them to work with.

o Have students chime in to share words that rhyme and can be incorporated in your class rhyme.

o Once you have created a few rhymes, you can make a class book that students can refer to during their free reading time.

MODIFICATIONS: If students need help with memorizing or reading the rhymes or chants, provide copies of the chant so they have instant access to the text.

TIPS: Some teachers complain that they don't know how to keep up with the rhymes and chant charts. One way to combat this is to use clothes hangers to hang the charts and store them. You can also post them around the room in a particular area so kids can access them during their small group center time, where they work on activities independently.

ANCHOR STANDARD ADDRESSED

CCSS.ELA-LITERACY.CCRA.SL.I — Prepare for and participate effectively in a range of conversations and collaborations with diverse partners, building on others' ideas and expressing their own clearly and persuasively.

41. Poetry

MATERIALS NEEDED

- Poem written on a chart

RATIONALE: Using poetry to teach students reading fluency and rhyming is an excellent strategy to incorporate during the morning meeting. Poetry has been shown to help increase student vocabulary and the ability to read fluently. Poetry is also a genre that is often overlooked during reading instruction. It is, however, a perfect genre to showcase orally during your morning meeting routine.

PREP

Carefully select a poem that reinforces concepts or skills that are being taught in the classroom. Write the poem down on a chart.

PROCEDURE

o Let students know that you will be reading a poem and that their job is to listen.

o Review your listening routine from activity #21 (page 58) if necessary.

o Always indicate a purpose for students as they are listening to the poem. You can have them listen for rhyming words, particular vocabulary words, nouns, pronouns, etc.

o After sharing the poem, ask students comprehension questions to build a purpose for reading.

MODIFICATIONS: Students may need help with recognizing rhyming words or vocabulary definitions. Have guiding questions ready ahead of time to help scaffold.

TIPS: Develop a routine for sharing poetry with your class. Ensure that the poems you pick focus on skills you want to reinforce with your class. Poems can be used to teach varied literacy skills such as rhyming, alliteration, fluent reading, robust vocabulary, personification, and the list goes on. One good poem can be used to teach many skills.

CCSS.ELA-LITERACY.CCRA.SL.6 — Adapt speech to a variety of contexts and communicative tasks, demonstrating command of formal English when indicated or appropriate.

42. Read Aloud

MATERIALS NEEDED

- Story to read aloud

RATIONALE: Research has indicated that read alouds provide an excellent opportunity for students to solidify important literacy skills, including comprehension and vocabulary building, identifying genre and story elements, and strengthening writing skills. They also foster listening comprehension, which is essential for improving vocabulary and sentence structure.

PROCEDURE

- Begin your read aloud by setting a purpose for the students. (This can include teaching a comprehension strategy or story element).

- Inform students that as they are listening to the story, they will need to use their listening skills. (Refer students back to activity #21, Listening Skills, page 58).

- As you focus on different components in the story, be direct and explicit in your examples from the text. Pause and discuss the idea or concept that you are focusing on.

- Use thinking aloud, or meta-cognition (sharing your thought process), to share examples from the text that relate to the standard or topic you are pulling from the text.

- Always end your read aloud by asking students questions that allow them to solidify the strategy or topic you explored during the read aloud.

MODIFICATIONS: Choose books that are appropriate to student need. Ensure that children clearly hear the story and see the pictures, if the book has them.

☛ **TIPS:** Read the story several times before the read aloud session so you are aware of when you will use a teaching point during a section of the text. You can use sticky notes or flags with notes on them to write the questions you will ask students during certain points in the story.

ANCHOR STANDARD ADDRESSED

CCSS.ELA-LITERACY.CCRA.R.2 — Determine central ideas or themes of a text and analyze their development; summarize the key supporting details and ideas.

43. Big Books

MATERIALS NEEDED

- Big book story
- Highlighting tape, sticky notes, or sentence frames

RATIONALE: Having larger books that students can interact with is a great way to model reading strategies with kids. Big books are interactive and full of clear details. You can do so much more when sharing big books than when you are working with a standard size book. For instance, you can use highlighting tape to emphasize words or ideas you want to focus on. Kids love interacting with big books, too.

PROCEDURE

o Share your big book on a stand or a designated area where you can display and interact with the book.

o Set the purpose for the reading (such a vocabulary or sentence structure skill) before you start.

o As you read, emphasize the skills you want to teach to students. You can do this by using different tools like highlighting tape, sticky notes, or sentence frames.

o The pictures/illustrations in big books provide an opportunity to discuss details and text features. Key in on these elements as you share the book.

o Always end your big book session with guiding questions for students to answer in order to reinforce the importance of reading comprehension.

🏴 **TIPS:** Provide books and topics that are appropriate to your students' needs and interests.

ANCHOR STANDARD ADDRESSED

CCSS.ELA-LITERACY.CCRA.R.7 — Integrate and evaluate content presented in diverse media and formats, including visually and quantitatively, as well as in words.

44. Audio Books

MATERIALS NEEDED
- Chart paper or whiteboard
- Markers
- Audio book

RATIONALE: Often, classes use listening centers during independent time. Modeling the activity as a whole group is a great way to teach the procedure and expectations. Listening to audio books during morning meeting provides an opportunity to model what listening to text looks and sounds like. Students can listen to text at reading levels two to three grades higher than their independent reading level; thus, listening to audio books allows students to comprehend complex texts to build comprehension and vocabulary.

PREP
o Choose the audio version of the book you want to share with students.

o Test your audio equipment before starting the lesson. I have observed many lessons where audio difficulties cause a lesson to go awry. Have a backup available just in case. Preparation is key! Set a purpose for students as they listen to the text.

PROCEDURE
o Write the objective/purpose for the session on a chart or whiteboard.

o Play the audio book. You can give the students the text to follow along with, project the text, or just have students listen to the text. This will all depend on the instructional level of your students and your objective.

o Conclude by asking students comprehension questions regarding the story they are listening to. A simple technique is to ask who, what, when, where, and how questions.

o Use the chart paper to capture student responses.

MODIFICATIONS: Choose audio texts that meet the educational and social needs of your students.

Provide support with accessing the technology to listen to the audio book.

ANCHOR STANDARD ADDRESSED

CCSS.ELA.LITERACY.CCRA.R.I0 — Read and comprehend complex literary and informational texts independently and proficiently.

45. Reader's Theater

MATERIALS NEEDED

- Student copies of reader's theater script
- Camera/recording equipment

RATIONALE: Students enjoy performing. Reader's theater provides an awesome opportunity for them to do so while working on their reading fluency and comprehension skills. Morning meeting provides an intimate, stress-free environment for students to perform reader's theater. It also is a perfect environment, because students have set rules for listening and speaking during the morning meeting routine.

PROCEDURE

o Explain to students that they will be performing a reader's theater script.

o Ask students if they have ever participated in reader's theater.

o Take any and all contributions.

o Remind students that when they perform, they want to make sure that they speak clearly and read with fluency so they engage their listeners.

o Explain that each student will have a part and they will be responsible for reading/performing that part.

o Assign parts to students.

o Give students time to practice their lines.

o You may allow students to make hats/costumes to bring their part to life.

o Once students are familiar with their parts, have them perform their lines.

o You can record and share with students. Students love seeing themselves on camera.

MODIFICATIONS: Modify reading lines and parts to ensure each student in the class has a part in the reader's theater experience. If students need help with their lines, provide this support. This activity may span a couple of morning meetings. Allow students time to be familiar with their lines and comfortable sharing.

ANCHOR STANDARDS ADDRESSED

CCSS.ELA-LITERACY.CCRA.SL.1 — Prepare for and participate effectively in a range of conversations and collaborations with diverse partners, building on others' ideas and expressing their own clearly and persuasively.

CCSS.ELA-LITERACY.CCRA.SL.4 — Present information, findings, and supporting evidence such that listeners can follow the line of reasoning and the organization, development, and style are appropriate to task, purpose, and audience.

CCSS.ELA-LITERACY.CCRA.SL.6 — Adapt speech to a variety of contexts and communicative tasks, demonstrating command of formal English when indicated or appropriate.

46. Alphabet Beat

MATERIALS NEEDED

- Alphabet chart
- Created beat or beat/song that you find online
- Audio recording device

RATIONALE: The first step in learning to read is to fluently recognize the letters of the alphabet and their sounds, which is also an IEP goal. This activity helps build this automaticity in letter recognition, which is essential.

PROCEDURE

o Display your alphabet chart.

o Read the letters of the alphabet with your class.

- Tell students that today they are going to create an alphabet beat.

- Ask students if they know what a beat is.

- Take any and all contributions.

- Tell students that a beat is a type of rap. Explain that your class will be creating their own beat for the alphabet.

- Share a sample alphabet beat from the Internet.

- Work with the class to create an original alphabet beat.

- Record your beat and play it occasionally to practice with the class.

MODIFICATIONS: To ensure total participation, provide assistance with repeating the beat with students who need this scaffold.

ANCHOR STANDARD ADDRESSED

CCSS.ELA-LITERACY.CCRA.SL.I — Prepare for and participate effectively in a range of conversations and collaborations with diverse partners, building on others' ideas and expressing their own clearly and persuasively.

47. Phonics Rock

RATIONALE: Phonics is the building block of decoding, and possessing basic phonics skills is an IEP goal. Students must have a strong phonics background in order to read fluently. This activity provides opportunities for students to practice their phonics skills by rhyming.

PROCEDURE

o Ask students if they know what rhyming means.

o Have students share their ideas.

o Take any and all contributions.

o Explain that rhyming words have the same ending sound.

o Share a few quick words that rhyme.

o Say two words and ask kids if they rhyme or not.

o Share a few more examples of word pairs. Ensure that some rhyme and some do not rhyme.

o Put the words cat, hat, fat, and mat on the board.

o Share a rap using a 2/3 count: "The fat cat sat on the mat."

o Tell students they will be creating their own phonics rap with the rhyming words they brainstorm together.

o Have students share words that rhyme with different ending sounds you want to focus on.

o Take up to four rhyming words for each ending sound.

o Ask the class to come up with a rhyme using all four words.

o Repeat with other ending sounds.

MODIFICATIONS: Provide scaffolds for students who are having trouble coming up with rhyming words. You can provide words and have them identify the word that does not rhyme to help teach them the skill.

TIPS: It may take some time for kids to come up with rhymes that make sense. Continue to practice this skill as necessary until students can do it seamlessly.

ANCHOR STANDARDS ADDRESSED

CCSS.ELA-LITERACY.CCRA.SL.1 — Prepare for and participate effectively in a range of conversations and collaborations with diverse partners, building on others' ideas and expressing their own clearly and persuasively.

48. Morning Story

MATERIALS NEEDED
- Story to share

RATIONALE: Sharing stories during morning meetings is a great way to settle students in. It provides the opportunity for students to enjoy stories in a familiar environment. This will help build a love of reading in students.

PROCEDURE
o Let students know you will be sharing a story this morning.

o Tell students the topic of the story or what the story is about.

o Set a purpose for the reading by asking students to think of questions they have as you are reading.

o Share the story.

o Ask students if they have any questions about the story.

o As students share their questions, respond as appropriate.

o Finish the activity by asking students to share with a partner what they enjoyed most about the story.

o Call on volunteers to share what they enjoyed most.

o Ask students to share some stories that they like to read or have read to them.

o Close by discussing how important it is to read for enjoyment.

MODIFICATIONS: If students need help with coming up with questions, provide this scaffold.

☛ **TIPS:** Picking the right stories to share for morning story is very important. Take into account social skills, concepts, or seasons and holidays that will interest students. Remember the focus on the morning story is reading for enjoyment. Pick books that will accomplish this goal.

CCSS.ELA-LITERACY.CCRA.R.l0 — Read and comprehend complex literary and informational texts independently and proficiently.

49. Letter Writing

MATERIALS NEEDED

- Chart with features of a friendly letter
- Chart paper
- Markers

RATIONALE: The intimate setting of morning meeting provides a great teaching environment to practice friendly letter writing.

PROCEDURE

- Ask students if they have ever written a letter.
- Tell students that today the class will be writing a letter to a chosen person. You may choose to write to a recent class visitor, principal, other teacher on campus, etc.
- Share the chart with the features of a friendly letter.
- Tell students you will be using the friendly letter features chart as a model.
- On chart paper, go through the process of writing the letter. Continue to use your chart as a model.

- Solicit student help as you write the letter. Students can help with spelling, choosing words, punctuation, salutations, etc.

- After the letter is composed, reread it with the class to get the final seal of approval.

- Have a student(s) deliver it to the recipient.

MODIFICATIONS: To ensure total participation, ensure you solicit responses from all students as you compose the letter.

ANCHOR STANDARD ADDRESSED

CCSS.ELA-LITERACY.CCRA.W.4 — Produce clear and coherent writing in which the development, organization, and style are appropriate to task, purpose, and audience.

50. Crossing the Midline

MATERIALS NEEDED

- Music
- Online video with midline crossing activities (optional)

RATIONALE: As an early childhood educator, I always include midline-crossing activities, which involve reaching across the middle of the body using arms and legs of the opposite side, in my classroom activities. Crossing the midline is often an occupational therapy goal in IEPs. Research notes that if students have difficulty crossing the midline, they often have struggles with reading and writing. This activity provides a fun and interactive way to practice the skill.

PROCEDURE

- Let students know that they are going to practice some exercises.
- Turn on the music and model the exercises you want students to follow.
- Walk around and help students who are having difficulty with the exercises.
- After doing the midline crossing activities, talk with kids about the importance of doing the exercises.
- Have students share which exercise they enjoy doing the most.
- As students become more proficient in the exercises, you can incorporate more midline activities.
- If students have difficulty with the activities, consult with your occupational therapist so they can provide further tips on how to help students with the skills.

TIPS: There are many midline-crossing activities that you can use. Search online and you can find hundreds of examples. There are even some online videos that you can follow along with to do your midline exercise activities.

CCSS.ELA-LITERACY.CCRA.SL.I — Prepare for and participate effectively in a range of conversations and collaborations with diverse partners, building on others' ideas and expressing their own clearly and persuasively.

51. Reading Buddies

MATERIALS NEEDED

- Student copies of reading log
- Books
- Soft music (optional)

RATIONALE: Reading buddies provide an opportunity for younger students to practice their reading skills. As students listen to books being read to them, comprehension is also reinforced. Reading buddies support friendships and connections for students.

PROCEDURE

o Pair students up with a reading buddy from another classroom.

o Let the buddies know their job is to read together and log the books they are reading on their reading log.

- Pass out the reading logs.

- Provide time for buddies to read together.

- When reading buddy time concludes, have the pairs turn in their reading logs so you can pass them out the next time they read together.

MODIFICATIONS: If students have difficulty working in pairs, provide an alternative arrangement.

TIPS: Reading buddies can be very successful if you ensure you have a strong commitment on the part of both the special education and general education teacher. Take the time to discuss the reading logs and what you want students to share on them, such as the name of the book, pages read, and summary. Finally, you may consider playing soft music to create a peaceful ambiance.

ANCHOR STANDARD ADDRESSED

CCSS.ELA.LITERACY.CCRA.R.I0 — Read and comprehend complex literary and informational texts independently and proficiently.

52. Fluency

MATERIALS NEEDED

- T-chart with columns labeled "Fluent" and "Non-fluent"
- Marker
- Chart paper
- Reading selection

RATIONALE: We know that reading fluency is correlated to reading comprehension. We also know that students have to be taught how to read fluently. This activity will provide that platform, as well as an opportunity to practice the IEP goal of reading with fluency and accuracy in a group setting.

PROCEDURE

- Ask students if they know what reading fluently means.

- Take any and all contributions.

- Let students know that they will be working on reading fluently during morning meeting.

- Share the fluency chart.

- Tell students you are going to read a passage. The first time you are going to read fluently and the next time you are going to read without fluency.

- Let them know their job is to share what they notice.

- Read the passage fluently.

- Next, read the passage without fluency. Pause and stumble, or read like a robot.

- Ask students to share what they noticed between both readings.

- Record their responses on the T-chart in the appropriate area.

- Read the shared passage together as a class with fluency.

- Close by reminding students what fluent reading sounds like by sharing the responses they provided on the T-Chart.

MODIFICATIONS: Provide passages at different reading levels to meet the needs of the learners.

TIPS: Ensure that you talk about expression, rate, and tone when discussing fluency. If students do not share these ideas when they share be sure to evoke them into the conversation.

53. The Big 5

MATERIALS NEEDED

■ Big 5 poster

RATIONALE: Reading is a very concise science. From reading research, we know that reading instruction is composed of five big ideas. Those ideas are phonemic awareness, phonics, fluency, vocabulary, and comprehension. To ensure student reading is developed, these components must be included during reading instruction. Students with reading IEPs will typically have components of the big 5 in their goals. This activity will serve to support those goals.

PROCEDURE

o Ask students why reading is important.

o Take any and all contributions.

o Write student responses on the board.

o Tell students that when teaching reading, there are five big components.

o Share the big 5 poster with the class.

o Tell students that the activities you share during morning meeting support the big 5.

o Let students know that you will highlight the area of the big 5 you are covering when you introduce a new activity.

 TIPS: This activity should be taught early on in your morning meeting routine. You will want to highlight the area of the big 5 you are covering when teaching your reading activities during morning meeting. This will help you in understanding which strand of the big 5 your kids are comprehending and which areas you need to focus more attention on.

ANCHOR STANDARD ADDRESSED

CCSS.ELA-LITERACY.CCRA.SL.I — Prepare for and participate effectively in a range of conversations and collaborations with diverse partners, building on others' ideas and expressing their own clearly and persuasively.

54. Word Walls

MATERIALS NEEDED
- Word wall with letters A to Z
- Index cards
- Tape or stapler to add your words to the word wall
- Markers

RATIONALE: Word walls have been around for a long time. They have passed the test of time because of their ability to help students during reading and writing activities by providing a permanent place for high frequency words. They also help students build vocabulary as they learn new terminology and add it to the word wall.

PROCEDURE
- Find a place in your classroom to build your word wall. You can use a white board, bulletin board, etc.
- Before adding a word to the word wall, ensure that you go over the meaning and spelling so kids gain automaticity with the words.
- Write the new word on an index card.
- Practice the words by chanting them and spelling them before adding them to the word wall.
- Place the words in a prominent area and size so students can easily access them.
- Add words weekly. Typically add no more than two or three per week.

MODIFICATIONS: Provide assistance for students who may have trouble with viewing the word wall. Provide portable or abbreviated word walls depending on student need.

☛ **TIPS:** There is no right or wrong way to build a word wall. Construct a word wall that will best support your students with reading and writing activities. Ensure the word wall is accessible for students so they can interact with it. You can also consider having students make portable word walls that they can readily use. Finally, be very selective about what goes on your word wall. Place only those high leverage words that students will need to use.

ANCHOR STANDARD ADDRESSED

CCSS.ELA-LITERACY.CCRA.SL.I — Prepare for and participate effectively in a range of conversations and collaborations with diverse partners, building on others' ideas and expressing their own clearly and persuasively.

55. Vocabulary

MATERIALS NEEDED
- Vocabulary cards with definitions
- Paper
- Pencils

RATIONALE: The number one predictor of student success is vocabulary development, which is often an IEP goal. This activity provides an opportunity to teach vocabulary in a safe and interactive environment, and for students to build their vocabulary and comprehension.

PREP
Prepare vocabulary cards with pictures and words for the vocabulary you want to teach to students. These vocabulary words can be based on a story you are going to share or an academic activity you will be completing.

PROCEDURE
- Start by sharing the vocabulary cards with students.
- Read the definition of the vocabulary word.
- Split students into groups.
- Students have the option to draw a picture of the vocabulary or act it out.
- Allow students to practice.
- Have groups share their drawings or skits for the vocabulary word.
- Repeat with the next vocabulary word.
- Conclude the lesson by going over the vocabulary.

MODIFICATIONS: If students need assistance with acting out or drawing the vocabulary words, ensure you have this assistance available.

☛ **TIPS:** Be sure to pick pictures that have meaning for students. Also, make sure the words are large and bold so students can easily access them.

CCSS.ELA-LITERACY.CCRA.L.1 — Demonstrate command of the conventions of standard English grammar and usage when writing or speaking.

CCSS.ELA-LITERACY.CCRA.SL.1 — Prepare for and participate effectively in a range of conversations and collaborations with diverse partners, building on others' ideas and expressing their own clearly and persuasively.

56. Sign Language

MATERIALS NEEDED

- Pictures of signs

RATIONALE: There are many benefits in teaching sign language to children who can hear. It helps to build vocabulary and language skills and provides a means to communicate. Students who have difficulty with communicating can use sign language to support their IEP communication goals.

PREP

o Research the signs you want to teach to your students.

o You can think about basic signs to communicate needs (bathroom, help, thank you, please, hello, what?, etc.).

o There are numerous online videos that can show you how to do the signs.

PROCEDURE

o Model the first sign and have students practice.

o Correct any student mistakes immediately. You don't want them learning the sign the wrong way.

o You can also post pictures of the signs in the morning meeting area as a reference guide.

o Teach no more than one sign per class period.

o Continue practicing it until the kids master it.

MODIFICATIONS: Students may need multiple opportunities to practice the sign before mastering it. Be sure to provide this scaffold.

☛ **TIPS:** Always practice the signs before you teach them to kids. It is also helpful to talk to someone who knows sign language so they can help you. I will never forget how I thought I knew how to do a sign and showed it to my friend, who knows sign language. It appears I was holding one of my fingers incorrectly and was signing something not so nice. Take caution and always practice the signs before sharing.

CCSS.ELA-LITERACY.CCRA.SL.1 — Prepare for and participate effectively in a range of conversations and collaborations with diverse partners, building on others' ideas and expressing their own clearly and persuasively.

57. Repeat After Me

MATERIALS NEEDED

- Direction cards (optional)

RATIONALE: Often students with autism have difficulty following multistep directions. Following multistep directions is often an IEP goal. This activity provides an opportunity to practice this skill in a game-like environment. Following verbal directions are part of the listening and speaking standards; thus, practicing this skill will help students in other language arts areas.

PROCEDURE

o Tell students that they are going to play a listening and speaking game.

o Tell them that their job is to listen carefully and do what you say.

o Start with a single-step direction like, "Raise your hand and say hello."

o The next multistep direction should be more complex, like "raise your hand, tap your foot, and say hello."

o Continue to increase the level of complexity each time.

o Observe students as they play the game. You can assess who will need more practice with this skill.

MODIFICATIONS: Observe which students need additional support in following multistep directions, and provide extra support during other times of the day. You can also provide students with cards and pictures to support the steps you are having them follow.

TIPS: A good way to ensure this activity goes off without a hitch is to write down exactly the directions you want students to repeat. You can sprinkle in vocabulary, directional words, math concepts, etc., to make the activity more rigorous and cross-curricular.

CCSS.ELA-LITERACY.CCRA.SL.I — Prepare for and participate effectively in a range of conversations and collaborations with diverse partners, building on others' ideas and expressing their own clearly and persuasively.

58. Comprehension

MATERIALS NEEDED
- Chart paper
- Markers
- Reading selection
- Paper
- Pencils

RATIONALE: We read in order to comprehend text. Comprehension is the focal point of reading instruction. This activity provides students with a fun and genuine strategy they can use to comprehend any text. Students with comprehension goals in their IEP can apply the strategy taught in this activity to build their comprehension.

PREP
o Write the word "Visualization" on a piece of chart paper. Draw a picture of an individual with a thought bubble and a picture inside it.

PROCEDURE
o Tell students that you are going to teach them a comprehension strategy.

o Ask students if they know what the word "visualization" means.

o Take any and all contributions.

o Share the visualization chart.

o Tell students that visualization is depicted in the picture. It means making a picture in your mind as you are reading.

o Tell students that you are going to practice this skill.

o Read a short passage.

o Use metacognition to talk about what you see in your head after reading the text.

o Draw what you discussed on a piece of chart paper.

o Tell students that they will now get a chance to practice visualization.

o Read another short passage.

o Give students paper and pencil and have them draw what they visualized after hearing the text.

o Allow students to share their drawings.

o Conclude the lesson by asking students how they will use visualization to help them comprehend text.

o Allow students to share their responses.

MODIFICATIONS: Provide assistance with drawing or coming up with ideas for students as necessary.

TIPS: Be very selective in the passages that you share for the model and practice. Ensure they will be robust enough that students will have something to draw. When you are modeling the strategy, go overboard with your metacognition example. Bring your thinking to the forefront as a model for students on the process that goes on in your mind to help you relate all the key details of the text.

ANCHOR STANDARDS ADDRESSED

CCSS.ELA.LITERACY.CCRA.R.I0 — Read and comprehend complex literary and informational texts independently and proficiently.

CCSS.ELA-LITERACY.CCRA.SL.I — Prepare for and participate effectively in a range of conversations and collaborations with diverse partners, building on others' ideas and expressing their own clearly and persuasively.

59. Who, What, When, and Where

MATERIALS NEEDED

- Chart paper
- Markers
- Story to read aloud
- Student copies of worksheet

RATIONALE: As students are reading, you want them to be thinking. So many kids are word callers and cannot tell you what they have read about once they are done. This strategy serves as a reminder to kids to think when reading and lets them know what type of things they need to remember as they are reading.

PREP

- Write "Who?" "What?" "When?" and "Where?" on your chart paper. Each of the words should be separated into boxes that you can fill in as you model the strategy.

- Prepare worksheets with the words "Who?" "What?" "When?" and "Where?" written in separate boxes.

o Preview a story that you are going to share with the class. Ensure it has all of the components necessary to complete the chart.

PROCEDURE

o Tell students that when they are reading, they need to be asking themselves questions about the text.

o Tell them that you are going to model how to do this.

o Share the chart you made with students.

o Tell students that you are going to read a story and fill in each box as you are reading.

o Read the story aloud and fill out the appropriate boxes.

o Review your filled-in chart after you have finished the story.

o Tell students that you have made sheets for them to match the chart.

o Tell them that as you are reading stories during morning meeting, sometimes they will fill in their charts along with you to practice comprehension.

MODIFICATIONS: Allow students to draw their responses if they are not able to write them.

☛ **TIPS:** Draw pictures along with words to model for students so that they can use either mode to record their responses.

ANCHOR STANDARDS ADDRESSED

CCSS.ELA.LITERACY.CCRA.R.10 — Read and comprehend complex literary and informational texts independently and proficiently.

CCSS.ELA-LITERACY.CCRA.SL.1 — Prepare for and participate effectively in a range of conversations and collaborations with diverse partners, building on others' ideas and expressing their own clearly and persuasively.

Chapter 5

STRATEGIES FOR SKILLS DEVELOPMENT IN SCIENCE AND MATH

The morning meeting provides a great platform to reinforce or teach science and math skills. What makes this time of day and structure so perfect is that you can informally assess student learning and determine which skills students have mastered and which skills need re-teaching. This helps to hone in your small group instruction to meet the individual needs of your students.

This chapter focuses on engaging activities you can incorporate in your morning meeting to teach addition, subtraction, graphing, problem solving, the scientific method, and other important skills. The 20 strategies shared have been used in classrooms successfully and have been found to be engaging and effective.

60. What's the Weather?

MATERIALS NEEDED

- Book about weather
- Weather poster with labels for sunny, cloudy, rainy, snowy, and windy, with pictures to illustrate each
- Laminated chart labeled "Today's Weather Is," with days Monday through Friday underneath to write in

RATIONALE: Students have a natural interest in nature and their surroundings. Tracking the weather helps to build weather vocabulary and science observation skills.

PROCEDURE

- o Tell students that you are going to read a story about weather.
- o Tell students their job is to think about the different types of weather shared in the book.

o After reading the story, ask students to share the different types of weather they learned about in the book.

o Tell students that as a class, you will be tracking the weather each day.

o Share the weather poster and laminated weather chart.

o Go over the different types of weather on the chart.

o Ask students what type of weather they are having today.

o Record the day's weather on the appropriate spot on the chart.

MODIFICATIONS: Provide scaffolds if students have difficulty identifying the weather types.

☛ **TIPS:** This activity can be very rewarding as a job for students. You can assign a classroom meteorologist who daily tracks the weather for a week. Their job would be to share the weather when you call on them.

ANCHOR STANDARDS ADDRESSED

CCSS.ELA-LITERACY.CCRA.SL.I — Prepare for and participate effectively in a range of conversations and collaborations with diverse partners, building on others' ideas and expressing their own clearly and persuasively.

NEXT GENERATION SCIENCE STANDARDS

K-ESS2-I — Use and share observations of local weather conditions to describe weather patterns over time.

MS-ESS2-5 — Collect data to provide evidence for how the motions and complex interactions of air masses results in weather condition.

61. Calendar Skills

MATERIALS NEEDED

- Calendar
- Calendar numbers in different colors or shapes

RATIONALE: Calendar time offers the opportunity to practice many diverse math skills. For instance, you can work on patterning by using different colors for shapes for the calendar numbers and skip counting when you count the days on the calendar.

PROCEDURE

- Determine what your calendar routine will be.
- It is important to follow the same routine daily so kids can easily follow the routine.
- Determine if you are going to do an AB, ABB, ABA, ABC, etc., pattern.
- You can have students guess the pattern each day as you add the new calendar number.

o You can also have them predict the next two to three patterns on the calendar as you fill in more of the calendar.

o You can also have students skip count the numbers as you complete the calendar.

MODIFICATIONS: If students are having trouble with patterns, you can provide math manipulatives like pattern blocks or snap cubes to assist them.

☛ **TIPS:** Ensure your calendar and calendar numbers are large enough so students can view them. Prepare the pattern shapes and questions you will ask regarding patterns, skip counting, etc., before your calendar routine so it flows seamlessly.

MATHEMATICAL PRACTICE ADDRESSED

CCSS.MATH.PRACTICE.MP5: — Use appropriate tools strategically.

62. Months and Seasons

MATERIALS NEEDED

- Book about the four seasons
- Chart labeled "Winter," "Spring," "Summer," "Fall"
- Markers

RATIONALE: Morning meeting provides an opportunity to have rich conversations regarding the different seasons and the months that they fit in. Children build vocabulary and practice categorization skills when completing this activity.

PROCEDURE

o Tell students that you are going to read about the four seasons.

o Ask students if they can name the four seasons.

o Take any and all contributions.

o Tell students that their job is to listen for the names of the four seasons as you read the book.

o After reading the book, show students the chart with the four seasons labeled.

o With prompting and support, brainstorm with students what the weather is like during each season, and during which months the season falls. Write what you come up with on the chart.

o After the chart is completed, post it in the class.

MODIFICATIONS: Students may need prompting and support to brainstorm the characteristics of each season. Be sure to have prompting questions prepared.

☛ **TIPS:** For a successful lesson, read the book you will share beforehand to ensure there is enough information provided about each season to support discussion. You may also need to read a couple of books and extend this lesson across several sessions to complete the chart.

CCSS.ELA-LITERACY.CCRA.SL.1 — Prepare for and participate effectively in a range of conversations and collaborations with diverse partners, building on others' ideas and expressing their own clearly and persuasively.

63. Holidays

MATERIALS NEEDED

- Book about different holidays around the world
- Chart labeled "Let's Celebrate"
- Books, online video resources, etc.
- Markers
- Presentation boards

RATIONALE: Teaching students about holidays that are celebrated around the world provides an opportunity for them to embrace different cultures as well as treasure their own cultural traditions.

PROCEDURE

- This activity is best taught during the winter when there are many different holidays to explore.

- Start by reading a book about different holidays. You can spread this across several days and read about a different holiday tradition each day.

- As you read each book, add the holiday to the chart labeled "Let's Celebrate."

- After you have read about all the holidays, have students pick a holiday they would like to research.

- Pair students to research different holidays.

- Let them know they will share what they have learned about the holiday during a future morning meeting.

- Provide books, online video resources, etc., for students to use for their research.

- Students should prepare notes for their presentation on a presentation board. They can include pictures to make the board more engaging.

- Provide each group 5 to 10 minutes to present their holiday.

- You can finish the activity by having a cultural day where kids can try different foods and listen to music from the countries explored for each holiday.

MODIFICATIONS: Pair students up according to ability so that each group has balance. Provide additional support as necessary to complete the project and present.

TIPS: I have used this activity for years and it is always a big hit. I have had parents come in to share their traditions. I have created a lighted bulletin board with images for each holiday explored and I have had a potluck luncheon with foods from each country explored. You can make this activity as big or small as you desire.

ANCHOR STANDARDS ADDRESSED

CCSS.ELA-LITERACY.CCRA.SL.1 — Prepare for and participate effectively in a range of conversations and collaborations with diverse partners, building on others' ideas and expressing their own clearly and persuasively.

CCSS.ELA-LITERACY.CCRA.SL.6 — Adapt speech to a variety of contexts and communicative tasks, demonstrating command of formal English when indicated or appropriate.

64. Sorting Activity

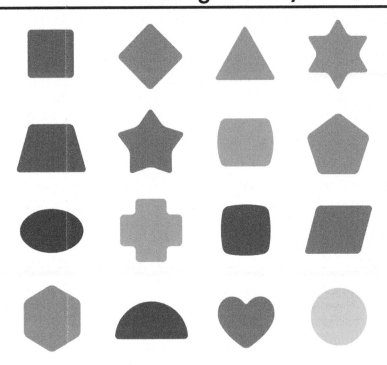

MATERIALS NEEDED

- Two hula hoops
- Items to sort

RATIONALE: The ability to sort and classify is important in building number sense and is often an IEP goal. This activity provides a classroom activity that brings sorting and classifying to a magnified scale.

PROCEDURE

- Tell students that they are going to sort and classify objects according to their attributes.

- Tell them that you will share different objects with each child and their job is to work together as a class to sort like objects together.

- Show the students the two overlapping hula hoops.

- Let them know that they will need to place objects in the appropriate hula hoop to classify.

- Give each student a few objects.

- Set the time for 10 minutes and let students classify the objects.

- Provide prompting and support as needed.

- When the timer goes off, talk to students about the objects sorted.

- See if any objects need to be moved to another spot.

- You may also choose to have some objects that do not fit at all and need to be eliminated.

- Repeat the activity as often as you wish to introduce different attributes to sort.

MODIFICATIONS: Provide assistance and support for students who may be having difficulty with classification.

☛ **TIPS:** When you are providing support, be sure to ask students questions to guide their choices of categorizing. This will provide valuable information regarding the students' understanding of classification.

ANCHOR STANDARDS ADDRESSED

CCSS.ELA-LITERACY.CCRA.SL.I — Prepare for and participate effectively in a range of conversations and collaborations with diverse partners, building on others' ideas and expressing their own clearly and persuasively.

MATHEMATICAL PRACTICE ADDRESSED

CCSS.MATH.PRACTICE.MPI — Make sense of problems and persevere in solving them.

65. Mental Math

MATERIALS NEEDED

- Online videos on mental math strategies
- White board
- Marker

RATIONALE: The ability to solve mathematical problems with automaticity and precision is important when building number sense. This activity will support students' ability to calculate without using paper and pencil.

PROCEDURE

o Watch online videos that teach mental math strategies that align with the math concept you want to focus on.

o Share a math problem on the white board.

o Tell students that their job is to solve the problem in their head.

o Tell students that solving the problem in their head means that they will not write the problem down, or use counters or other objects, but will figure the problem out on their own.

o Have students share their answers.

o Continue this process with increasingly difficult math problems.

o Release students to go with a partner to solve math problems on white boards.

o As you are observing and providing support, make note of which students need more support in solving problems.

o Bring the class back together and have volunteers share what they found interesting about solving mental math problems.

o Continue this routine as necessary to support students' ability to master mental math strategies.

MODIFICATIONS: Some students may struggle with mental math problem solving. If students need the additional support of counters, provide them and scale them away as students become more proficient.

TIPS: Teaching students mental math strategies can be challenging. You want to ensure that you are providing adequate support so students can grasp the concepts. Solving mental math problems with precision and accuracy takes a lot of practice. Be patient and continue to have students practice this skill.

MATHEMATICAL PRACTICE ADDRESSED

CCSS.MATH.PRACTICE.MPI — Make sense of problems and persevere in solving them.

66. Birthday Math

MATERIALS NEEDED

- Large bar graph with months on the X axis and numbers on the Y axis.
- Student names on paper to place on the bar graph
- Markers
- Student birthday information

RATIONALE: Students love activities that are personal and have special meaning for them. Birthday math activities accomplish this by providing them an opportunity to solve math problems based on themselves. There are many birthday math activities that you can share. Two that are very popular are birthday graphs (graph the months of the year that class members were born), and writing word problems based on student birthdays. Example: John is five, how old will he be in two years?

PROCEDURE

o Let students know you are going to collect data to share how many birthdays are in each month.

o Share large birthday graph.

o Tell students they will be placing their name on the graph in the month they were born.

o Start with January and have students come up to place their name on the graph in the month they were born.

o Once everyone has placed their name on the graph, ask students what they notice about the graph.

o Ask the following questions: Which month has the most birthdays? Which month has the least birthdays? Which month as the same amount of birthdays?

o Ask other questions that relate to your data.

o Conclude the lesson by reminding students that we use bar graphs to display data in a way that it can be easily viewed.

o Display the finished products in the morning meeting area for student reference.

MODIFICATIONS: Have alternative assignments available for students who do not celebrate birthdays or need additional support to complete activities.

☛ **TIPS:** Adequate preparation will be key in ensuring students get the most out of the birthday math activities. The graphing activity offers a plethora of opportunities to compare numbers, predict outcomes, etc.

MATHEMATICAL PRACTICE ADDRESSED

CCSS.MATH.PRACTICE.MP1 — Make sense of problems and persevere in solving them.

67. Number of Days in School

MATERIALS NEEDED

- Cashiers receipt roll or other object to track the number of days in school
- Markers

RATIONALE: Keeping track of the number of days in school helps to build numeracy in students. This activity provides a quick routine for practicing math concepts like skip counting.

PROCEDURE

o Start tracking the number of days in school on the first day of school.

o You can use cashiers tape, number lines, index cards, etc., to write the numbers.

o Each day you will write the number of days you have been in school.

o Once you have enough numbers you can skip count them, look for patterns, etc.

MODIFICATIONS: To ensure total participation, have supports in place so all students can contribute to the number of days in school activity. You can do this by having one-on-one time to complete the task for students as needed.

TIPS: Set a reminder to track the number of days in school. If you forget a day or are absent, place those numbers up as soon as possible to keep the tracking going. Many teachers have a big celebration to commemorate the 100th day of school. You can commemorate the 100th day or any other day that you deem appropriate.

MATHEMATICAL PRACTICE ADDRESSED

CCSS.MATH.PRACTICE.MP6 — Attend to precision.

68. Linking Chains

MATERIALS NEEDED

- Linking chains

RATIONALE: Math manipulatives like linking chains are a great source for problem solving. Many students benefit from using tactile objects to represent math concepts. Linking chains are often used to count and sort.

PROCEDURE

- o Before allowing students to explore with the chains, you want to set a purpose for their exploration with the manipulatives. Determine what math concept you want to model using linking chains.

- o Always model the proper use and care of the materials before allowing students to use them.

- o Upon completion of the math sorting or counting activity, have students share what they learned with the group.

MODIFICATIONS: Some students may have difficulty with linking the chains. Have alternative objects for their use or provide support.

🐾 **TIPS:** Linking chains can be used to teach many math concepts. You want to ensure you have a lesson in mind that the chains will work with. Pre-sort the chains so you can easily pass them out and get started with the activity.

MATHEMATICAL PRACTICE ADDRESSED

CCSS.MATH.PRACTICE.MP1 — Make sense of problems and persevere in solving them.

69. Pattern Blocks

MATERIALS NEEDED
- Picture of a tessellation to share with the class
- Pattern blocks

RATIONALE: Teaching students about tessellations, or tilings in nature and in the environment, is a great entry into the teaching of geometry. Observing patterns and tessellations helps students begin to explore the angle properties of shapes. This activity provides a great introduction to tessellations and gets kids to start thinking about shapes and their qualities.

PROCEDURE
- Tell students that they are going to be creating a tiling pattern and then painting it.
- Show a picture of a tessellation.
- Explain that tessellation or tiling occurs when we cover a surface with a pattern of flat shapes so there are no overlaps or gaps.
- Tell students that you are going to give them three minutes to explore the classroom to look for tessellations.
- Give students time to explore.
- Call students back together and have them share the tessellations they found in the classroom.
- Tell students you are going to give them each a set of pattern blocks.
- Explain that their job is to make a tessellation. Let them know that after their tessellation is complete, they will be painting it so that you can display it in the classroom.
- Provide time for students to work on their tessellation projects.
- Walk around and provide assistance as needed.
- After students have completed their tessellation with the pattern blocks, provide the tools needed to paint the tessellation.
- This activity may span across a few days.

o As students complete their artwork, display them on a board titled "Tessellation Art."

MODIFICATIONS: If students need help constructing their tessellation patterns, provide this assistance. This can come in the form of providing a sample tessellation that they can copy or expand upon. Also, be sure to provide help for students that may need assistance with painting their tessellation pattern once it is complete.

TIPS: Ensure you have pictures around the classroom with sample tessellation patters so students have models to help them when constructing their own tessellation.

MATHEMATICAL PRACTICES ADDRESSED

CCSS.MATH.PRACTICE.MPI — Make sense of problems and persevere in solving them.

CCSS.MATH.PRACTICE.MP5 — Use appropriate tools strategically.

70. Money Activity

MATERIALS NEEDED

- Play money
- Toys and trinkets for class store

RATIONALE: Providing an opportunity for students to learn to earn money and spend it wisely is an important life skill. This strategy will help you incorporate money skills in your classroom rewards system.

PROCEDURE

- o Let students know that you will be opening a classroom store.
- o Explain that in order to buy something from the store, students have to exhibit proper behavior during morning meeting.
- o Show students the items available in your classroom store.
- o Let students know that you will be giving out money weekly to students that behave appropriately during morning meeting.

○ Decide how much you want students to earn each week.

○ At the end of each week, distribute the money to students who have earned it.

○ Allow them to purchase items in the store.

○ They will also have the option of saving their money to buy more expensive items.

MODIFICATIONS: If students do not have a grasp of how to spend and save money, provide more explicit instruction on this concept.

☛ **TIPS:** Have items of different price ranges for kids. Make sure the items in your store are of value to students.

MATHEMATICAL PRACTICE ADDRESSED

CCSS.MATH.PRACTICE.MP1 — Make sense of problems and persevere in solving them.

71. Science Journal

MATERIALS NEEDED

- Chart paper
- Markers
- Science journals for each student
- Pencils
- Object(s) to observe

RATIONALE: There is often not enough time to teach science during the normal school day. This activity allows students to explore science during morning meeting in a nonthreatening group environment.

PROCEDURE

- Ask students if they know why scientists keep notes on their observations.
- Take any and all contributions.
- Share that scientists keep notes on their observations because they want to mark their observations and record their findings.
- Let students know that they will be keeping a science journal to record their findings.
- Explain that they will write and draw scientific observations in their science journals.
- On a chart, model how to draw and write about an observation in the science journal.
- Be direct and explicit in your model.
- Ask students if they have any questions about what the expectation is for their science journals.
- Take any and all questions.
- Distribute science journals and pencils, and release students to write about observations in their journals.
- Provide scaffold and support as needed as you walk around.
- Have student volunteers share their journal pages.

MODIFICATIONS: Allow students to draw their observations if they have difficulty with writing.

☛ **TIPS:** You can have students observe an ant farm, a growing plant, butterflies, etc. Your science journal can be a notebook or a few pieces of paper stapled together.

ANCHOR STANDARDS ADDRESSED

CCSS.ELA-LITERACY.CCRA.SL.I — Prepare for and participate effectively in a range of conversations and collaborations with diverse partners, building on others' ideas and expressing their own clearly and persuasively.

CCSS.ELA-LITERACY.CCRA.W.8 — Gather relevant information from multiple print and digital sources, assess the credibility and accuracy of each source, and integrate the information while avoiding plagiarism.

72. Nature Walk

MATERIALS NEEDED

- Chart paper
- Markers

RATIONALE: Taking a break from the classroom environment to walk and observe nature is a nice way to avoid monotony and provide an opportunity for students to become more aware of their surroundings. It is also a nice way to bring harmony and calm to students.

PROCEDURE

o Let students know that they are going to go on a nature walk.

o Set the purpose by asking students to pay attention to their surroundings and to be prepared to share what they see.

o As you are taking the nature walk, talk to students about the sounds and sights.

o Have students touch the leaves and other objects.

o You can collect some items on your nature walk to display in the classroom.

o Upon returning, have students share what they noticed while on the nature walk.

o Record their observations on chart paper.

MODIFICATIONS: If you have students in wheelchairs, have aides or parent support to ensure all students have the opportunity to go on the nature walk.

☛ **TIPS:** You will want to go out ahead of taking students on the nature walk to be prepared for any changes outside. For example, maybe the playground has been watered or there are tree branches down from a storm. You can also scope out the path you want to take students on and determine stops of interest.

ANCHOR STANDARD ADDRESSED

CCSS.ELA-LITERACY.CCRA.SL.I — Prepare for and participate effectively in a range of conversations and collaborations with diverse partners, building on others' ideas and expressing their own clearly and persuasively.

73. Math Stories

MATERIALS NEEDED

- Chart paper with "CUBES Strategy" written on it.
- Markers

RATIONALE: Students need to be aware of how to solve math story problems. Sharing their strategies for story problems during morning meeting provides this opportunity in a community environment.

PROCEDURE

o Tell students that you are going to be sharing some math story problems to solve.

o Tell students that the strategy they will be using to solve the word problems is called "CUBE."

o Share the CUBE Strategy chart.

o Tell them that C stands for "Circle the important numbers," U stands for "Underline the question," B stands for "Box the key terms," E stands for

"Evaluate the question and eliminate unnecessary information," and S stands for "Solve and check your work."

o Go over each letter and what it stands for.

o Share a math word problem.

o Use the chart to solve each step of the problem.

o Tell students that you are going to have them solve a problem with you.

o Solve a second math problem, calling on students to help you solve each step of the problem.

o Close the lesson by asking students what they learned about the CUBE strategy.

MODIFICATIONS: If students are having difficulty with the CUBE strategy, provide one-on-one modeling. You can also have them master one step at a time.

TIPS: Always pre-write your word problems and ensure that they will work with the strategy. Try to use student's names or other items of interest in your word problems to build interest.

MATHEMATICAL PRACTICE ADDRESSED

CCSS.MATH.PRACTICE.MP1 — Make sense of problems and persevere in solving them.

74. Measurement

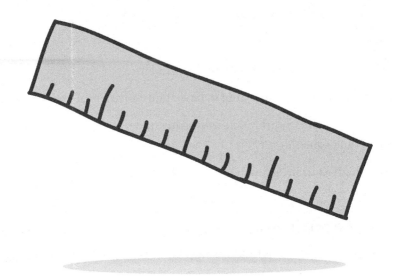

MATERIALS NEEDED

- Chart paper with diagram of a 12-inch ruler
- Rulers (enough for each student)
- Student copies of worksheet with listed items and pictures of the items for students to measure (crayons, pencils, eraser, etc.)
- Pencils

RATIONALE: Understanding measurement helps students with an important life skill. Understanding how to estimate the length of common objects is something we are called on to do almost every day. Measurement helps students understand expressions of property (how long, how short), and it also helps them use standard units of measurement. Reinforcing measurement during morning meeting is a nice way to reinforce these skills.

PROCEDURE

- Ask students what type of tools we can use to measure items.
- Take any and all contributions.
- Talk about each measuring tool the students shared.

- Let them know that they are going to be using rulers today to measure common objects in the room.

- Share your diagram of a ruler.

- Explain how to use a ruler to measure.

- Model measuring a pencil for the class.

- Provide each student with a ruler and a worksheet with selected items to find and measure in the classroom.

- Release students to measure objects in the room.

- Bring students back together.

- Call on students to share the measurements of the items on the worksheet.

- Close the lesson by asking students to share what they enjoyed most about the measurement activity.

MODIFICATIONS: Provide additional assistance for students who need more scaffolds in understanding how to measure items. Have an aide work one on one with students who need this level of support.

TIPS: Your worksheet should have pictures of the items that you want students to measure. You can also set up measurement stations in several areas of the room. Each station can have all of the items being measured to help cut down on chaos.

MATHEMATICAL PRACTICE ADDRESSED

CCSS.MATH.PRACTICE.MP5 — Use appropriate tools strategically.

75. Graphing

MATERIALS NEEDED
- Chart paper
- Marker

RATIONALE: Children build mathematical reasoning when they work on graphing. Graphs allow students to gather information and ask questions. This activity provides an opportunity to share graphing as a class.

PROCEDURE
- Ask students what type of graphs they are familiar with.
- Take any and all contributions.
- Tell students that they are going to make some class graphs that will help them learn more about each other.
- Ask students what their favorite color is.
- Using the chart paper and marker, create a bar graph that shows the information gathered.
- Ask students questions about the graph. Examples: Which color do most students like? Which color is the least favorite?
- Each day of the week, ask different graphing questions that focus on student interests.
- Display the graphs in the morning meeting area for reference.

MODIFICATIONS: Provide assistance for students who may have difficulty sharing what their interests are. Ensure you get the information from parents if necessary so all students are represented on the graph.

TIPS: You can do the graphing activity as a check-in for the morning. Have a question posted and students can come in and signify their preferences.

CCSS.ELA-LITERACY.CCRA.SL.I — Prepare for and participate effectively in a range of conversations and collaborations with diverse partners, building on others' ideas and expressing their own clearly and persuasively.

CCSS.MATH.PRACTICE.MP3 — Construct viable arguments and critique the reasoning of others.

76. Classroom Patterns

MATERIALS NEEDED
- Paper
- Pencils

RATIONALE: The ability to recognize patterns has a high correlation with general intelligence. Recognizing patterns in chaos helps students in mathematics and other subjects. Identifying and creating patterns also contributes to social development as students make predictions about what may come next.

PROCEDURE
- Tell students that they are going to go on a pattern hunt in the classroom.
- Remind students what a pattern is by showing them a few basic patterns.
- Share one pattern in the classroom to get everyone started.
- Tell students their job is to find as many patterns as they can and report back to the group.
- Each student should be a given paper and a pencil to track the patterns that they find.
- Release students to search for patterns.
- Have students share the patterns that they found with the group.
- Conclude the lesson by reminding students that patterns can be found all around. Tell them to continue to look for patterns throughout the day outside and around the school.

MODIFICATIONS: Pair students if they will need additional support in observing patterns.

TIPS: Add items in the classroom that have patterns to help support more interaction. You can also post pictures of butterflies, birds, etc., to provide more examples of patterns to discover.

CCSS.ELA-LITERACY.CCRA.SL.I — Prepare for and participate effectively in a range of conversations and collaborations with diverse partners, building on others' ideas and expressing their own clearly and persuasively.

CCSS.MATH.PRACTICE.MPI — Make sense of problems and persevere in solving them.

77. Shapes and Angles

MATERIALS NEEDED

- Chart showing right, acute, straight and obtuse angles (copied from student worksheet) (page 243)
- Marker
- Student copies of worksheet
- Pencils

RATIONALE: Geometry is an important math concept that students need to master. Often students find geometry challenging as they move to more advanced grade levels. This activity provides a fun and engaging way to explore geometry.

PROCEDURE

- Tell students that they are going to be learning about different angles.
- Explain that when lines of shapes interact, they make different types of angles.
- Share the angles chart.
- Go over each angle type with students.
- Share a chart that is a model of the worksheet you will provide for students.
- Model finding a few of the angles in the classroom using the chart as a guide.
- Tell students that they will have time to explore the classroom to find right, acute, straight, and obtuse angles.
- Tell students they will use the worksheet with the angles as a guide to find angles in the classroom.
- Tell students the expectation will be to share the angles they find with the class.
- Distribute the worksheets and pencils and release students to find angles.
- Have students share the angles they found with the class.
- Close the lesson by reminding students what the angle types are.

MODIFICATIONS: Pair students who need additional support. Have students only find one angle type if they need this scaffold.

➤ **TIPS:** You can provide more examples of the different angle types by bringing additional items into the classroom to support this activity.

ANCHOR STANDARD ADDRESSED

CCSS.ELA-LITERACY.CCRA.SL.I — Prepare for and participate effectively in a range of conversations and collaborations with diverse partners, building on others' ideas and expressing their own clearly and persuasively.

MATHEMATICAL PRACTICE ADDRESSED

CCSS.MATH.PRACTICE.MPI — Make sense of problems and persevere in solving them.

78. Telling Time

MATERIALS NEEDED

- Chart with information on how to read an analog clock and digital clock (see page 244)
- Judy Clocks or other practice clocks for each student or pair of students.

RATIONALE: The ability to tell time helps students gain independence and strengthens their ability to be self-regulated. It also increases self-confidence and eases anxiety when they are able to gauge how much more time they have to spend on an activity or be at school.

PROCEDURE

- Tell students that you will be referring to the clock throughout the morning meeting.
- Ask students if they are familiar with how to read a clock.
- Take any and all contributions.
- Explain that there are two types of clocks.
- Share the chart that explains the different clock types.
- Go over the chart with the class.

- Using a Judy Clock, practice reading the time. (You want to start reading time by the hour and build up depending on student knowledge.)

- Also, share digital clock times and practice reading the time.

- Tell students that throughout the week, they will be practicing reading time during morning meeting.

MODIFICATIONS: If students need more practice with time, provide Judy Clocks for them to work with. You can also make a time-reading center that they can explore.

⚑ TIPS: Telling time can be challenging for some students. This might be an activity that will be necessary for students to practice for a while. You can also find some interactive online time-reading games that students can explore.

MATHEMATICAL PRACTICE ADDRESSED

CCSS.MATH.PRACTICE.MP5 — Use appropriate tools strategically.

79. Skip Counting

RATIONALE: Skip counting is a basic math skill that should be mastered in the primary grades. Skip counting can be infused in many of the morning meeting routines to help support grasping this essential skill.

PROCEDURE

o Skip count the number of days in school.

o When skip counting, tell students what measure you are skip counting by (2, 5, 10...)

o Play skip counting games and practice skip counting as a start to your math section of morning meeting.

o The game can involve the girls skip counting by twos and the boys skip counting by fives.

o You can also have children clap as they skip count to bring in movement.

MODIFICATIONS: Provide one-on-one teaching of skip counting for students who are having difficulty mastering the concept.

TIPS: Skip counting should become automatic for students. Encourage skip counting whenever you have items to count. You want this strategy to become ingrained in student thinking.

ANCHOR STANDARD ADDRESSED

CCSS.ELA-LITERACY.CCRA.SL.I — Prepare for and participate effectively in a range of conversations and collaborations with diverse partners, building on others' ideas and expressing their own clearly and persuasively.

MATHEMATICAL PRACTICE ADDRESSED

CCSS.MATH.PRACTICE.MPI — Make sense of problems and persevere in solving them.

Chapter 6
BONUS ACTIVITIES

A variety of activities and strategies can be used during the morning meeting routine. I have gone over strategies that support community building, social development, English language arts, and math. This chapter will focus on 21 additional activities and strategies that can be easily implemented to support skill building, academic skills, and team building. This chapter is full of fun-filled activities that foster independence and fun. Students should enjoy the morning meeting routine. It is a time to establish friendships, build understanding, and learn important social and academic skills. This chapter is a smorgasbord of activities that you and your kid are sure to enjoy.

80. Total Physical Response (TPR)

RATIONALE: When they involve their bodies in the learning process, kids are more likely to retain what they are learning. Using Total Physical Response (TPR), a language learning approach where students use physical movements to remember vocabulary and concepts, is a nice way to allow students to practice what they are learning.

PROCEDURE

o When introducing a new movement for a vocabulary word or concept, start by modeling the movement for students.

o Share the word/concept and the movement that goes along with it.

o Have students repeat the word and the movement.

o Continue practicing until students can do the movement fluidly.

MODIFICATIONS: Help students with the movement if they are not able to do it on their own.

TIPS: Teach the movements in manageable chunks. Do not try to teach too many concepts at one time. I have found that teaching no more than four to five movements at a time is manageable.

CCSS.ELA-LITERACY.CCRA.SL.I — Prepare for and participate effectively in a range of conversations and collaborations with diverse partners, building on others' ideas and expressing their own clearly and persuasively.

81. Let's Celebrate

MATERIALS NEEDED

- Cheer cards (cards with pictures of different cheers. For example, disco cheer, rodeo cheer, roller coaster cheer, etc.)

RATIONALE: A great way to build community and rapport is to celebrate as often as possible. This helps bring your community together in a positive way.

PROCEDURE

o Tell students that you are going to celebrate the wonderful things that you have accomplished during morning meeting with a cheer.

o Ask students what they think the class should celebrate.

o Take any and all contributions.

o Pick a couple of the students' ideas to cheer about.

o Have the students randomly pick a cheer card.

o Perform the cheer with the class.

MODIFICATIONS: To ensure all students have a part in the celebrations, set standards to include all learners.

TIPS: Focus celebrations on student effort and achievement. This will ensure all students feel valued and included in the classroom celebrations. Celebrations should be well calculated and organized. Celebrations can be as simple as a cheer for new learning or a full-blown classroom party. Celebrate academic and social development milestones.

ANCHOR STANDARD ADDRESSED

CCSS.ELA-LITERACY.CCRA.SL.I — Prepare for and participate effectively in a range of conversations and collaborations with diverse partners, building on others' ideas and expressing their own clearly and persuasively.

82. Hand Jive

MATERIALS NEEDED
- Music (optional)

RATIONALE: Students with difficulty with fine motor development can face challenges with other life tasks, like getting dressed, writing, and using eating utensils. Activities like hand jive help to build motor skills, a goal for students in occupational therapy.

PROCEDURE
o Let students know that you are going to be teaching them a clapping game.

o Model the steps to the clapping game for students.

o An easy one to start with is Miss Mary Mack.

o Have student pairs practice Miss Mary Mack.

o As students are practicing, go around to monitor and offer support.

o You can play music and have students practice other clapping patterns that you model.

MODIFICATIONS: Give students simple clapping patterns if they are having trouble completing the clapping patterns. You can also provide pictures of the movements for the clapping patterns if students need visual cues.

TIPS: There are numerous clapping games and patterns that you can teach students. Conduct an online search for clapping games to find more ideas.

ANCHOR STANDARD ADDRESSED
CCSS.ELA-LITERACY.CCRA.SL.I — Prepare for and participate effectively in a range of conversations and collaborations with diverse partners, building on others' ideas and expressing their own clearly and persuasively.

83. Sound Off

MATERIALS NEEDED
- Vocabulary cards (as needed)
- Fluency passages (as needed)

RATIONALE: IEP goals often involve listening and speaking. The ability to listen and comprehend what is being said is imperative for student learning. This activity allows students to practice their receptive language skills in a nonthreatening manner.

PROCEDURE
- Let students know you are going to teach them a fun listening game.
- Tell them the game is called "Sound Off."
- Tell them you will say a word or phrase and their job is to repeat it back.
- Practice this procedure using a few short words or sentences.
- You can use your vocabulary cards and have students repeat the word and its definition.
- You can also read fluency passages and have students repeat using intonation.
- Continue playing the game, but increase the complexity and length of the sentences/phrases you share.
- Once students get the hang of the game, have them practice being the teacher.
- This game can be played anytime you want to practice vocabulary or fluency.

MODIFICATIONS: Decrease the sentence lengths for students that need this scaffold.

TIPS: This activity works very well when you are introducing new vocabulary. You can have students repeat the vocabulary word and the definition. You can also use this strategy to practice procedures and rules.

CCSS.ELA-LITERACY.CCRA.SL.1 — Prepare for and participate effectively in a range of conversations and collaborations with diverse partners, building on others' ideas and expressing their own clearly and persuasively.

84. All Hands on Deck

MATERIALS NEEDED

- Puzzle pieces for two or more different puzzles, depending on your class size

RATIONALE: It takes a community to accomplish tasks. Most jobs in the future will require students to work in team environments. This activity supports this important skill.

PROCEDURE

o Tell students that they will be completing a task that will require the assistance of everyone in the class.

o Have a few puzzles that the class will be using their pieces to complete.

o Pass out puzzle pieces to everyone in class. (Be strategic when passing out the puzzle pieces, thinking ahead about which puzzle the piece will fit into).

o Tell them that each of them will have to work together to solve the puzzle.

o Have the class work together to find the matching pieces to their puzzle.

o Students will have to figure out which puzzle their piece belongs to.

o Once the puzzles are all completed, call the class back to group.

o Ask them what they found interesting about the activity.

o Take any and all contributions.

o Conclude by reminding students of the importance of working together to get all the puzzles completed.

MODIFICATIONS: Provide support for students who are having trouble finding their matching puzzle.

🢒 **TIPS:** You may have to work on this activity with your reading buddies if you do not have enough students in your homeroom to complete the activity. This works best when you have at least 2 or 3 different puzzles to complete.

You can also cut up Sunday comics and laminate them to make puzzle pieces.

CCSS.ELA-LITERACY.CCRA.SL.I — Prepare for and participate effectively in a range of conversations and collaborations with diverse partners, building on others' ideas and expressing their own clearly and persuasively.

85. Friendship Circle

MATERIALS NEEDED

- Book about friends (see page 233 for suggestions)
- Chart paper
- Markers

RATIONALE: The ability to make friends is an important social skill. This activity teaches students to think about the characteristics of a friend, which, in turn, will help them exhibit these social skills.

PROCEDURE

- Tell students that you are going to read a story about friendship.

- Tell them to think about the actions the characters take that make them a good friend.

- After reading the story, have students share what they learned about the characteristics of a good friend.

- Record student responses on chart paper.

- Create a new chart titled "How We Show Friendship."

- Brainstorm with students what being a friend looks and sounds like.

- Conclude by re-reading the characteristics the class listed.

MODIFICATIONS: Provide extra support for students who are having trouble coming up with ideas to share.

TIPS: Be very selective in the book you decide to share. I have sometimes used books that show both positive and poor examples of friendship to build a contrast.

ANCHOR STANDARDS ADDRESSED

CCSS.ELA-LITERACY.CCRA.R.2 — Determine central ideas or themes of a text and analyze their development; summarize the key supporting details and ideas.

CCSS.ELA-LITERACY.CCRA.SL.I — Prepare for and participate effectively in a range of conversations and collaborations with diverse partners, building on others' ideas and expressing their own clearly and persuasively.

86. Oral Storytelling

MATERIALS NEEDED
- Chart paper
- Markers

RATIONALE: Students love telling stories about their lives. This activity allows students to talk about themselves, meet IEP goals to increase their oral processing, and practice other storytelling skills like sequencing, character development, and main idea.

PROCEDURE
o Tell students that they are going to have the opportunity to tell a story about their life.

o Tell students that you are going to model by telling them a story about your life.

o Tell a short story about an event in your life.

o After you complete your story, write the following on chart paper: "Characters, Setting, and Events."

o With the students, record on the chart the characters, setting, and events in your story.

o Tell students that they will be telling a story of their own.

o Let them know their story must also have characters, setting, and events.

o Pair students and let them know they will have two minutes to share their stories with a partner.

o Release student pairs to tell their stories.

o After two minutes, have partners change roles.

o Call students back together as a group.

o Call on a couple of volunteers to share their stories.

o With the class, go over the characters, setting, and events from the student stories shared.

MODIFICATIONS: Students can use setting cards as reminders if they are having trouble remembering what needs to be in their story.

☛ **TIPS:** As you teach other story elements (problem, solution, etc.) you can ask students to include them in their oral stories.

87. Task Cards

MATERIALS NEEDED
- Index cards

RATIONALE: Task cards provide an opportunity for students to practice skills and teachers to assess student mastery of standards and skills that have been taught. They can also be used as a spiral review or to revisit standards and skills that have already been taught.

PROCEDURE
o Determine which skills your students need to practice and reinforce.

o Create task cards with open-ended or multiple choice questions that relate to the skills and standards you want to review.

o On one side of the card, write the question stem.

o On the opposite side of the card, write the answer.

o Go over the task card with the student group.

o Read the question and have students respond.

o Always go over the correct answer with the kids.

o Pair students to complete task cards with a partner.

o Monitor students as they complete the task cards and provide support as needed.

MODIFICATIONS: Pair students accordingly so they can support one another. You can differentiate the questions asked to meet the individual needs of your students.

☞ **TIPS:** Use pictures and graphics to help make your task cards more engaging. If you are including multiple choice questions on your task cards, be sure that your responses are balanced so students have to think about their responses. You don't want your incorrect responses to be too easy to eliminate.

CCSS.ELA-LITERACY.CCRA.SL.I — Prepare for and participate effectively in a range of conversations and collaborations with diverse partners, building on others' ideas and expressing their own clearly and persuasively.

88. Theme Baskets

MATERIALS NEEDED

- Basket
- Several books on a chosen topic

RATIONALE: Reading multiple texts on a subject allows students to build knowledge and a wide range of understanding. Reading both fiction and nonfiction text provides an opportunity to see different sides to a topic, which builds comprehension.

PROCEDURE

- Determine which topic you want to build a theme basket for.
- Topics should be of high interest and should be able to support skills and standards that are important for student learning.
- Find multiple texts on the topic chosen. Include a balance of fiction and nonfiction texts on the subject. You can include magazine articles also.
- Once your basket is complete, present it to the class.

- Introduce the basket by letting students know that the basket contains multiple texts on the given subject.

- Share the text titles in the basket with the class.

- Let students know that you will be reading some of the texts in the basket during morning meeting.

- Let them know they can assess the basket to explore the books also.

- Each day, share a text from the basket with the class.

MODIFICATIONS: Include texts of different reading levels so all students can assess the texts.

☞ **TIPS:** Allowing students to explore the texts in the theme basket is the most powerful part of this strategy. Students will begin to develop a love for reading and exploring as they are given the opportunity to assess diverse texts on a topic. You can make your basket fancy and cute by adding labels and pictures. Make the basket very enticing so students are excited about the texts.

ANCHOR STANDARD ADDRESSED

CCSS.ELA-LITERACY.CCRA.SL.I — Prepare for and participate effectively in a range of conversations and collaborations with diverse partners, building on others' ideas and expressing their own clearly and persuasively.

89. Activity Cards

MATERIALS NEEDED

- Snowman Anchor Chart (see Example)
- Activity cards for students (activities can include how to draw or build a pattern, how to make a flower using pattern blocks)
- Pattern blocks
- Snap cubes
- Paper
- Pencils

EXAMPLE:

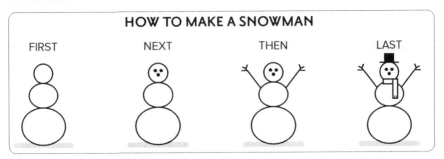

HOW TO MAKE A SNOWMAN

FIRST   NEXT   THEN   LAST

RATIONALE: Activity cards help build independence for students. Students learn to follow written directions to complete tasks, which is often an IEP goal.

PROCEDURE

o Tell students you are going to share a chart with instructions on how to draw a snowman.

o Share the chart.

o As you read each step on the chart, be very explicit in your actions.

o Have students follow along with you as you draw a snowman together.

o Tell students that they will be doing the same thing, but will use an activity card instead of a chart.

- Create activity cards on index cards that allow students to perform tasks independently.

- Pair students and have them work on an activity card.

- As they are working on the activity card, monitor and provide support as needed.

- After students have practiced their skills, bring students back together and discuss how the activity card activity went.

- Allow students to work on activity cards when you have independent work time in your class.

MODIFICATIONS: Provide more visuals if students are having difficulty with completing their task cards.

TIPS: Activity cards can be used for any subject and skill. Ensure the activity cards you create are engaging and include images. Review the steps on your activity cards to ensure they are sequential and readily assessable for student interpretation.

ANCHOR STANDARD ADDRESSED

CCSS.ELA-LITERACY.CCRA.SL.I — Prepare for and participate effectively in a range of conversations and collaborations with diverse partners, building on others' ideas and expressing their own clearly and persuasively.

90. Using Technology

MATERIALS NEEDED

- Technology (laptops, iPads, tablets, smartphone, etc.)
- Smart board, projector, or other device to display the activities for students

RATIONALE: Students are instantly engaged when they are given an opportunity to work with technology. Using technology in the classroom helps to raise their attention level, which, in part, increases retention.

PROCEDURE

o Find an educational application or interactive teaching website you want to share.

o Set up your smart board or other interactive display unit.

o Display the website with your class.

o Have the students interact with your presentation by building in interactive questions or having kids help to switch the pages or answer questions.

o If you have enough devices for the class, have the students engage with the site independently or in groups.

MODIFICATIONS: If students need assistance maneuvering the website or engaging with the technology, have these scaffolds available.

☛ **TIPS:** When working with technology, always test your devices before presenting. Also, have a Plan B in case technology fails. There are some neat ways to use Apple TV and your smartphone to project if you do not have an interactive board. See the appendices for more information.

ANCHOR STANDARDS ADDRESSED

CCSS.ELA-LITERACY.CCRA.SL.I — Prepare for and participate effectively in a range of conversations and collaborations with diverse partners, building on others' ideas and expressing their own clearly and persuasively.

CCSS.ELA-LITERACY.CCRA.W.6 — Use technology, including the Internet, to produce and publish writing and to interact and collaborate with others.

91. History Detectives

MATERIALS NEEDED
- Chart paper
- Markers

RATIONALE: The ability to think critically is essential for student growth. This activity allows students to formulate questions about historical events to build their understanding.

PROCEDURE
- Tell students they are going to act as history detectives.
- Explain that detectives work to solve mysteries, and one of the ways they solve the mysteries is by asking questions.
- Tell students that you are going to model for them how to ask questions like a detective.
- Share a story about an event in history.
- Create a History Detective chart (see page 245 for what to include).
- Fill in each blank on the chart. Allow students to help with the responses.
- The research portion may require that you take several days to complete the activity.
- Conclude the lesson by reminding students that detectives ask questions to come up with conclusions.
- Once the chart is complete, hang it in a prominent place for easy access.

MODIFICATIONS: Par down the activity to meet the needs of your students. You may only ask one question to start and build up to three as students become more proficient.

☛ **TIPS:** Be very selective in the historical event you research. You want to also make sure you know where to go to find the research for the questions that you ask.

CCSS.ELA-LITERACY.CCRA.SL.I — Prepare for and participate effectively in a range of conversations and collaborations with diverse partners, building on others' ideas and expressing their own clearly and persuasively.

CCSS.ELA-LITERACY.CCRA.SL.4 — Present information, findings, and supporting evidence such that listeners can follow the line of reasoning and the organization, development, and style are appropriate to the task, purpose, and audience.

CCSS.ELA-LITERACY.CCRA.W.6 — Use technology, including the Internet, to produce and publish writing and to interact and collaborate with others.

CCSS.ELA-LITERACY.CCRA.W.7 — Conduct short as well as more sustained research projects based on focused questions, demonstrating understanding of the subject under investigation.

92. Charades

MATERIALS NEEDED
- Index cards

RATIONALE: Creating motions for vocabulary words provides an opportunity to engage other senses in the learning process. Research has shown this helps with retention.

PREP
Prepare a list of vocabulary words on index cards.

PROCEDURE
o Tell students you are going to be teaching them a game called charades.

o Explain that charades involves using your body to make movements for vocabulary words.

o Read a vocabulary word from one of your prepared index cards.

o Share a movement for the card.

o Pull the next vocabulary card and have class volunteers share a body movement.

o Make the game more interesting by some students do movements and the class guess the word.

MODIFICATIONS: Provide assistance with coming up with movements for students that struggle with this. This ensures all students have an opportunity to participate.

🏴 **TIPS:** Charades can be played not only with vocabulary words, but to act out different behaviors, like showing happiness, sadness, excitement, etc.

ANCHOR STANDARDS ADDRESSED

CCSS.ELA-LITERACY.CCRA.L.4 — Determine or clarify the meaning of unknown and multiple-meaning words and phrases by using context clues, analyzing meaningful word parts, and consulting general and specialized reference materials, as appropriate.

CCSS.ELA-LITERACY.CCRA.SL.I — Prepare for and participate effectively in a range of conversations and collaborations with diverse partners, building on others' ideas and expressing their own clearly and persuasively.

93. Finish the Story

MATERIALS NEEDED

- Ideas to start your story

RATIONALE: Activities like Finish the Story provide opportunities for kids to think. They will be required to add information to a team story. This provides a great opportunity to think about story elements and put what they know into practice.

PROCEDURE

o Have the students sit in a circle.

o Let students know that they will be working as a team to create a story.

o Explain that each person will add to the story when it is their turn.

o Let students know that what they add must be open so that the next person can carry on the story.

o Start the story.

o The next person in the circle will add details to the story.

o Go around the circle, allowing each person a turn to add details.

o Once you have completed the story circle, ask students what they thought about your team story.

o Students will become more proficient with the activity each time you do it.

o This activity can be repeated as often as desired.

MODIFICATIONS: Some students may struggle with adding details when it is their turn. Readily provide coaching as necessary.

TIPS: Get together a set of story starters and tips before the activity begins. You can also provide some samples for students on ideas to add to the story for those that are having trouble.

CCSS.ELA-LITERACY.CCRA.SL.I — Prepare for and participate effectively in a range of conversations and collaborations with diverse partners, building on others' ideas and expressing their own clearly and persuasively.

CCSS.ELA-LITERACY.CCRA.SL.4 — Present information, findings, and supporting evidence such that listeners can follow the line of reasoning and the organization, development, and style are appropriate to the task, purpose, and audience.

94. Alternate Endings

MATERIALS NEEDED

- Story to Share
- Chart paper titled "How Can We Change the Ending?"
- Markers

RATIONALE: This activity provides an opportunity for students to work on their listening comprehension skills and their creative thinking skills. In order to create an alternate ending, they will have to understand the text and create logical alternative endings for the story. This requires higher levels of thinking and increased depth of knowledge.

PROCEDURE

- Let students know that you will be reading a fairy tale to them and that, as a class, they will be coming up with a different ending for the story.

- Explain that their job is to listen carefully so they are ready to think about ways to end the story.

- Read the story aloud to the students.

- Once you have finished the story, refer students to the chart.

- As a class, work together to write an alternate ending for the story.

- This will be messy work, so don't be afraid to cross out ideas and start over.

- Once you have drafted your alternate ending, share it aloud.

- Conclude by having students vote on their favorite ending—the new one they created or the traditional ending.

MODIFICATIONS: To encourage participation, you ask leading questions for all students and call on everyone to add ideas.

☛ **TIPS:** This activity can be very engaging when you are sure to pick a story that kids are familiar with. Chose a fairy tale they have heard before so they are not learning a new story to write an alternate ending for.

CCSS.ELA-LITERACY.CCRA.W.4 — Produce clear and coherent writing in which the development, organization, and style are appropriate to task, purpose, and audience.

CCSS.ELA-LITERACY.CCRA.SL.I — Prepare for and participate effectively in a range of conversations and collaborations with diverse partners, building on others' ideas and expressing their own clearly and persuasively.

95. If I Was Anywhere in the World

MATERIALS NEEDED

- Chart paper
- Markers
- Map, books, and pamphlets
- Internet access

RATIONALE: There is often not enough time in the day to teach social studies. This activity allows you to touch on social studies standards while teaching social skills.

PROCEDURE

- Ask students where they would go if they could visit any place in the world.
- Have each child share.
- Write their responses on the chart.
- As a class, vote on the top three or four (this will depend on the number of groups you will have) they would like to learn more about.

o Tell students that they are going to be put into teams to research their assigned country. Let them know they will need to find information about the people, famous landmarks, animals, and foods of their assigned country.

o Provide maps, books, pamphlets, and Internet access so teams can conduct research.

o Set students in groups to have time to research the country they are assigned. Release students to work on their assignment.

o Monitor and provide support as students work in their groups.

o This activity may span a week.

o Once teams have completed their research, have them share their findings with the class.

MODIFICATIONS: Have flexible grouping so all students have an opportunity to participate. If teams need modifications on their assignment, provide this option.

TIPS: The library and local travel agencies are good places to go to find resources for this activity. Your local AAA office can also be a good place to go for pamphlets and travel guides.

ANCHOR STANDARDS ADDRESSED

CCSS.ELA-LITERACY.CCRA.SL.I — Prepare for and participate effectively in a range of conversations and collaborations with diverse partners, building on others' ideas and expressing their own clearly and persuasively.

CCSS.ELA-LITERACY.CCRA.W.6 — Use technology, including the Internet, to produce and publish writing and to interact and collaborate with others.

CCSS.ELA-LITERACY.CCRA.W.7 — Conduct short as well as more sustained research projects based on focused questions, demonstrating understanding of the subject under investigation.

96. Favorite Things

MATERIALS NEEDED
- Chart paper
- Markers

RATIONALE: Students enjoy talking about the things they enjoy. This activity will spark conversation and also provide an opportunity to work on graphing skills.

PROCEDURE
- Tell students that you are going to take a poll about their favorite thing. (Limit this by asking for their favorite book, lunch, dinner, toy, movie, etc.)
- On a chart, write "My Favorite _____."
- Take student responses to the prompt.
- Record their responses on the chart.
- Tell students they are now going to make a bar graph to represent the information shared.
- With your class, create the bar graph on a chart.
- Have student volunteers color in the bar graph.
- Once the graph is complete, talk with students about what the chart shows.
- Conclude by asking students if they were surprised by the results.

MODIFICATIONS: If students need more practice reading graphs, provide this scaffold.

☛ **TIPS:** You can print images from the Internet to use as labels for the graph to make it more engaging. You can also do different types of charts if your students have mastered bar graphs.

CCSS.ELA-LITERACY.CCRA.SL.I — Prepare for and participate effectively in a range of conversations and collaborations with diverse partners, building on others' ideas and expressing their own clearly and persuasively.

97. Rain or Shine

MATERIALS NEEDED

- Pictures of different activities that relate to different types of weather. For example, snowboarding, hiking, or soccer-playing pictures.
- Chart paper with Venn diagram labeled "Rainy" and "Sunny"
- Markers
- Tape

RATIONALE: This activity promotes critical thinking skills. Students are required to justify their thinking regarding the probability, safety, and reasonability of doing an activity on a rainy or sunny day.

PROCEDURE

- Tell students you are going to play a picture game where you sort activities depending on if they can be done on a rainy day, sunny day, or both days.

- Share pictures with your students.

- Have discussions regarding where the pictures fit on the Venn diagram and why.

- Tape each picture under the respective side on the Venn diagram.

- If you have activities that can be done on either day, bring out discussion regarding why this is the case.

- To promote discussion, have students share their ideas with a partner before sharing aloud.

- Conclude the activity by looking at the complete Venn diagram and going over the choices.

- When you do this final review, you can change picture placement if the class thinks something needs to be moved.

MODIFICATIONS: If students need more processing time before they share, provide this scaffold.

TIPS: Ensure your Venn diagram is large enough to accommodate all the pictures that you are sharing. Also, be very strategic in the pictures you share. You want pictures that will cross over to both days so that you can have rich discussions.

ANCHOR STANDARD ADDRESSED

CCSS.ELA-LITERACY.CCRA.SL.I — Prepare for and participate effectively in a range of conversations and collaborations with diverse partners, building on others' ideas and expressing their own clearly and persuasively.

98. Fact or Fiction

MATERIALS NEEDED
- Chart paper
- Markers
- Statements to read (fact and fiction)

RATIONALE: Being able to distinguish fact from fiction is an important skill that students need to master. Students are exposed to both fiction and nonfiction texts. Understanding the characteristics of each genre can help them understand text features for each genre. This activity teaches the skill in a fun and engaging manner.

PROCEDURE
o On a chart, write the words "Fact" and "Fiction."

o Ask students to help you write definitions for both words.

o After you have written your definitions, tell students that they are going to practice identifying facts and fiction.

o Explain that you will be reading several statements, and their job is to determine if the statement is a fact or is fictional.

o Read statements to students and vote as a group on where the statement fits.

o After you have gone through all the statements, conclude the lesson by reviewing the definition of fact and fiction.

o You can extend the lesson by having students write their own fact and fiction sentences to share at a future morning meeting.

MODIFICATIONS: If students struggle with understanding fact and fiction, provide more examples. You can also share pictures as a way to cue students in on the differences.

TIPS: Make sure the examples you share are distinguishable as fact or fiction. You can find some very interesting ones, like statements about ligers or zonkeys. Kids will have fun discovering these things do indeed exist.

99. Sum It Up

MATERIALS NEEDED

- Chart paper
- Markers
- Short story to summarize

RATIONALE: The ability to summarize is imperative to building comprehension. This task allows students to summarize information orally, which will build their ability to summarize written information. When students summarize, they have to determine the most important ideas. Summarizing also helps students memorize details.

PROCEDURE

- Tell students that they are going to work on summarizing information.
- Draw a T-chart and write "Main Idea" and "Key Points."
- Explain that you will be reading a short story to students, and their job is to help you identify the main ideas and key points.
- Read the text aloud.
- Stop at key points in the story to note on the T-chart the main ideas and key points that are identified.

- Once you have completed the reading with the class, compose a summary of the text that was read.

- Involve students in the summary writing by having them share their ideas.

- Conclude the lesson by reading the summary.

MODIFICATIONS: Ensure all students are involved in the summarizing process by asking questions of all students. You can also use picture clues to help students remember what the main idea and key points are.

🏴 **TIPS:** You may need to remind students that a summary is about the key ideas and details in a text. Their opinions and feelings are not part of the summary. You can make a chart that distinguishes the differences in summarizing fiction and nonfiction. For fiction, summary focuses on characters, setting, problem, and solution. In nonfiction, the focus of the summary is the main idea, details from each section, and author purpose.

ANCHOR STANDARDS ADDRESSED

CCSS.ELA-LITERACY.CCRA.R.2 — Determine central ideas or themes of a text and analyze their development; summarize the key supporting details and ideas.

CCSS.ELA-LITERACY.CCRA.SL.I — Prepare for and participate effectively in a range of conversations and collaborations with diverse partners, building on others' ideas and expressing their own clearly and persuasively.

100. Bring It On

MATERIALS NEEDED

- Online example of debate
- Computer or projector
- Topic for debate
- Timer

RATIONALE: The ability to formulate an opinion based on facts and personal preferences is an important skill to hone in students. They will use it in their opinion writing and when formulating evidence to form their own personal opinions. This activity promotes creative thinking and the development of debating skills. It is performed in a safe group setting, which will help ease anxiety.

PROCEDURE

- Tell students that they are going to have a classroom debate.
- Ask students if they know what the word "debate" means.
- Take any and all responses.
- Explain that a debate is a discussion where you share reasons for and against an idea.
- Share a short online explanation of a debate. (There are numerous short online resources with this information.)
- Tell students that you are going to have a debate for or against having recess. (You can pick another topic if this one does not work for your class.)
- Split your class into two groups, for and against.
- Flip a coin to see which side will present first.
- Conduct your debate. (Decide on the number of rounds you want to go.)
- You will want to use your timer to set a limit on the time each side has to share.

- At the end of the debate, the class can vote on which side they think made the best points.

- Ask students what they liked about the debate.

- Tell students that debating is important because it teaches them to look at more than one side of an issue.

- Continue to practice debating as important issues arise in your classroom or on campus.

MODIFICATIONS: If students are not able to participate verbally in the debate, allow them to share pictures or respond with yes or no answers to debate questions.

☛ **TIPS:** Debating is a difficult skill for kids to master. You can help out by prompting students on what to say. You can also have them write down their thoughts so they are readily available to share.

ANCHOR STANDARDS ADDRESSED

CCSS.ELA-LITERACY.CCRA.SL.I — Prepare for and participate effectively in a range of conversations and collaborations with diverse partners, building on others' ideas and expressing their own clearly and persuasively.

CCSS.ELA-LITERACY.CCRA.SL.4 — Present information, findings, and supporting evidence such that listeners can follow the line of reasoning and the organization, development, and style are appropriate to the task, purpose, and audience.

Chapter 7
BRINGING IT ALL TOGETHER

Keeping Your Morning Meetings Fresh and Alive

We have just explored 100 strategies that you can use during your morning meeting routine. The strategies shared span across several different areas of focus. We discussed how to bring in movement, oral language, listening skills, and skills-based teaching. We did this by focusing on five main areas. The five areas covered include community building, social development, English language arts, social studies, and finally, math and science. Each of these areas can be highlighted during your morning meeting time to reinforce and teach important concepts and elicit student participation.

Students will learn those essential social skills of taking turns when talking, sharing, listening to others, and the list goes on and on. They will also learn to take responsibility for their learning. When you work in collaborative small group settings, kids can't hide and not participate. This structure will allow students who may be shy to find their voice and start to share their thoughts and ideas. Morning meeting also helps to review academic skills that are important for students to master. You can sprinkle in content teaching and scaffold skills development quite easily during your morning meeting routine. I have seen teachers work on spelling patterns, math patterns, and speech patterns in one short morning meeting session.

Morning meetings provide so many opportunities for students to take an active part in their learning community. Starting your day with a time of community building is essential for building a classroom culture that is collaborative and inclusive.

Community Building

Community building is one of the key benefits in using the morning meeting method. Your classroom community grows stronger each day you run your morning meetings. Students begin to bond and share the responsibility of ensuring the classroom runs well. You will soon see that the behaviors taught during morning meeting start to appear throughout the school day. The best way to accomplish this is to continually remind students of those skills as they interact inside and outside the classroom.

Community building also takes place when you discuss how all student opinions and ideas are important. That is why in each section it is reiterated to take any and all contributions. This action helps build community as all voices are heard.

It is also important that kids understand the classroom belongs to them and not just to the teacher. This is important to help kids become responsible for the care of the classroom community as they take on classroom jobs and have a hand in maintaining the order.

Motivation

One of the key community-building blocks is to increase the level of motivation your students have for learning. Motivation is a key indicator of a student's likelihood to persist in their learning. This is vital as academic standards increase and students are being held to much higher levels of learning. Persisting in learning tasks is often a struggle for students in special education. In fact, persistence in learning tasks is a challenge for all students. If we know that motivation plays a key part in student persistence, finding ways to motivate our kids is going to be important. There are three things you can do to motivate students to learn. They include the connecting, encouraging, and engaging.

Connecting

Students that are motivated see a connection in what they are learning and their own world. We have known for years that children thrive when they can make personal connections to the ideas that they are being taught.

I remember Madeline Hunter's model of teaching. Madeline Hunter is an educational guru on lesson planning. According to the Hunter model, we had to start each lesson with a set. This set included making a connection to students regarding why they needed to learn the particular information that was going to be presented.

My set was about the importance of learning to add numbers, because as adults, they will be required to shop for things like groceries and clothing. One of the math lesson sets I vividly remember was the following:

"Boys and girls, today we are going to learn addition. Addition is important to learn because, when you are an adult and go grocery shopping, it will be important that you know how to add. Let's say that you have $20.00 to spend on your grocery trip. You are picking all the items you need for the week. You continue to just throw items in the cart, not thinking about how the cost is adding up. You get to the checkout counter and the bill rings up to $43.00. You panic because you only have $20.00, and there is a line forming behind you with customers who are in a hurry to get home. You could have avoided this stress if you had added those items using mental math before going to the checkout counter. Now, you will have to put items back that you cannot afford to purchase, which will be embarrassing."

My students always got a kick out of this example. They had all been to the grocery store with their parents and could relate to such an experience.

Encouraging

Students who are motivated have teachers that serve as cheerleaders for their success and effort. They encourage student to take risks in their learning and provide words of encouragement when students show less effort. Make your classroom a place where learning is celebrated, learning is fun, and students are recognized for their achievements. You can display student work that exhibits care and effort. You can also consider giving awards for students' effort in the form of certificates or small tokens. Here are some classroom encouragement ideas you can consider:

o Student of the week

o Display stellar student work

o Recognize student achievement in your parent newsletter

o Positive calls home

Engaging

Students in classes that are engaging have higher motivation. Engaging classrooms have the following characteristics:

o Students have input in the learning tasks

o Lessons are differentiated

o Students have many opportunities to participate

o There are clear expectations for learning

o Grouping is flexible

o Classroom is student focused

o Class has game-like simulations

o There is a focus on student mastery

Intrinsic and Extrinsic Motivation

There are two different ways that students can show motivation. Some students are intrinsically motivated and others are extrinsically motivated. Intrinsic motivation is internal and extrinsic motivation comes from outside sources.

Here are the characteristics of intrinsically motivated students:

o Motivated to learn from within

o Finds learning pleasant

o Is curious about what they are learning

o Has goals for their learning

Here are the characteristics of students who are extrinsically motivated:

o Learns to achieve a reward

o Learns to avoid a punishment

We want to get our students to the point where they are intrinsically motivated. Here are some ideas to help promote intrinsic motivation in your classroom:

o Give students choice

o Celebrate success

o Provide tasks that students connect with

o Set rules for sharing so kids do not risk being embarrassed or shamed

o Don't use extrinsic rewards too often

o Celebrate student growth

Social Development

Social development is the building block of student's ability to function effectively. Students must learn how to manage stress and adversity so they can grow to be empathetic, trusting, and self-confident. Students, and even adults, can always benefit from reinforcing social skills. As we move further into the twenty-first century, students will be required to work more often in group settings. Most jobs require team planning and team problem solving. Think about Silicon Valley and how they structure their workplaces. Most of the breathtaking technology we now have resulted from group brainstorming sessions. Start building student understanding on how brainstorming and team building work during your morning meetings.

Some of the benefits of social development include:

o Being able to handle negative emotions

o Ability to develop healthy, satisfying relationships

o Being able to take part in group activities

Teaching Kids to Handle Stress

One great way to help kids handle stress is to teach them some strategies to use if they begin to feel stressed. The first thing is to help kids recognize when they are beginning to feel stressed. Here are some stress warning signs you can teach your kids so they can recognize that their behavior or feelings are stress related:

o My hands clench

o I grit my teeth

o My hands get sweaty

o My breathing becomes shallow

o My face feels warm

o My face turns red

o My fists are balled up

o I tap my feet or hands

o I fidget my body

Once kids can recognize the signals of stress, you want to teach them what to do to relieve the stress and why it is important to relieve their stress for a better learning experience. Here are some simple things kids can try:

o Take deep breaths

o Ask the teacher for a break

o Ask for a fidget or stress ball

o Ask for a drink of water

o Ask for a time out outside of the room

These few tips can really help kids begin to work on their stress-related behaviors and to relieve their stress in a positive manner. The above tips can be shared during morning meeting or in a one-on-one situation. I have seen students really internalize the process and show tremendous growth when taught these methods.

Yoga and Other Meditative Strategies

There has been a recent push for including yoga classes in our schools to help students manage their stress. Yoga in the classroom is a new concept at the writing of this book, but I anticipate that it will continue to build a following as schools become more aware of the challenges students bring to the classroom. Yoga is a perfect way to bring mindfulness and calm to students as they learn to self-manage their social and emotional health. Here are some the benefits of using yoga in the classroom:

o Increases student concentration

o Eases anxiety

o Increases student success

o Addresses diverse learning styles

o Relieves physical tension

o Relieves mental stress

o Provides strategies to being calm

o Increases student mindfulness when they are experiencing tension

English Language Arts and Social Studies

Building literacy skills requires that students spend time engaging with literature. During the morning meeting, you can share rich literature and model thinking and comprehension strategies. You can also provide opportunities for students to practice their reading fluency and their ability to figure out the meaning of unknown words. What is so special about teaching these skills during the morning meeting is again the ability to scaffold and re-teach as necessary.

Here are few reasons to teach language arts and social studies during morning meeting:

o Increases student focus

o Differentiates instruction

o Provides student models

o Scaffolds concepts

o Assesses student learning

Math and Science

As with English language arts, math and science concepts are also best taught when you can scaffold and provide opportunities for students to engage in the process. When you go over the calendar and have students skip count, you are building the numeracy and math fluency that will be necessary when students begin to learn more complex math concepts. Science teaching also ties in very well with the morning meeting framework. Students are able to discuss the scientific method and learn to observe their surroundings when they share their observations during the group setting.

Math and science concepts can be easily included during morning meeting. Here are a few benefits of adding the teaching of math and science to your morning meeting routine:

o Reinforces concepts

o Practices math facts

o Practices mental math

o Uses problem solving

o Discusses math in everyday life

o Observes patterns of nature

o Works collaboratively to problem solve

Repetition, Repetition, Repetition

One of the ideas that has come up continually in this book is the idea of repetition, including the repetition of skills, and its role during the morning meeting routine. Repetition is especially important for students with learning deficits and cognitive disabilities. This repetition does not hurt students who do not have these deficits, it only reinforces the information for them and they begin to internalize the concepts at a much deeper level.

Zone of Proximal Development

As you reintroduce or re-teach concepts, be cognizant of what your students already know so that each time you reintroduce a topic, you bring in new information to take kids to the next level. This style of teaching goes back to Lev Vygotsky's theory of the zone of proximal development. This theory has been around for many years, but still rings true today. Lev Vygotsky was a Soviet psychologist who observed children and discovered that children follow adult examples until they are finally able to take on tasks without support or help. The zone of proximal development, is in essence, what a child can do alone with the help and support of an adult or other expert. During your morning meeting scaffolds, you want to keep very clearly in mind where you can start to take support away and allow kids to do more of the work. This may look like having kids come up with rhyming words or having students think of ways to solve a problem. Your job is to start to wean them from support until they can complete the activity independently.

Metacognition

Metacognition, or thinking about our thinking, is another very important concept to employ during your skills-based teaching. We model metacognition when we make our subconscious processes conscious. This is often used to illustrate what you think about when you solve a math problem, write a story, or answer a comprehension question. This strategy works especially well during morning meeting because many of the activities that take place during morning meeting require that the teacher model the skills for students before they try them on their own. Following are a few tips to use when modeling metacognition with your students:

o Think aloud. Make your thinking visible by clearly explaining your thinking process.

o Activate prior knowledge. Stop and discuss what you already know about a subject or topic.

o Monitor. Read a word incorrectly and go back and correct it. Model that the word does not make sense so you have to go back and fix it.

o Question. Model the questions you ask yourself to self-monitor when you are reading.

The key to modeling metacognition is not to leave out any of the steps you take in coming to or drawing a conclusion when performing a task. One way I prepared for a metacognition lesson was to work my way through a task.

I wrote down everything that goes through my head as I complete the task. I found this helped me not forget any important steps in the process that I wanted to share with students.

Now What?

Once you've spent a few months tweaking and modifying your morning meeting routine to meet the individual needs of the students in your classroom, you may find the need to add some more structures to keep kids actively engaged and excited about morning meetings. The one caution here is not to take away those essential tenants of the morning greeting: sharing that schedule for the day and spending time working on a skill for the day. These components are essential to maintain structure and predictability that students strive in. There are, however, a few things you can think about adding to bring some new life to your meetings.

Parent Involvement

When it is feasible, invite parents to take part in your morning meeting routine. It will help to build community and will also help your students showcase their learning with their parents. You can schedule quarterly parent-involved morning meeting activities. Some activities to consider inviting parents to include:

o Cultural celebrations

o Academic celebrations

o Reader's theater productions

o Unit review events

o Classroom art gallery

o Community engagement projects

Afternoon Meeting

Often teachers indicate that they just don't have enough time in their morning meeting routine to get to all the things they want to get to. One thing you can consider is to have a weekly afternoon meeting. I have often seen teachers hold an afternoon meeting on Friday. During this afternoon meeting, they go over the key points of the week, celebrate student effort and achievement, and set the stage for the upcoming week.

What I really like about these weekly afternoon meetings is that it sets the tone for students and lets them end their week on a high note. Many of our kids go home to not-so-positive home lives. Having this afternoon meeting to look forward to offers an opportunity for students to enjoy celebrate their learning successes for the week.

The afternoon meeting format should be an abbreviated morning meeting. You will not need to have the greeting, but you will have a goodbye routine. This may look like students giving each other a high five or a pat on the back before they end their week of learning together. Some teachers sing a goodbye song as a culminating activity.

Key questions to ask yourself when planning your afternoon meeting are:

1. What do I want my students to leave this week knowing?

2. What were the key concepts or skills taught this week?

3. How will we celebrate student growth for the week?

4. Who do I want to celebrate their efforts this week?

5. What token do I want students to leave with this week?

6. How do I want students to leave feeling this week?

7. How will students know they had a successful week?

8. What concepts for next week do I want to let students know about?

Once you have answered the questions, you can develop your plan of execution. You can choose to focus on any of the questions posed. These are just starting points to give you ideas of what information you want to share with your students during the afternoon meeting.

If you implement question five, you can think about small tokens to celebrate student growth. Some teachers give out money that kids can use to buy things in a classroom store once they have earned enough. Others give out pencils or other small trinkets. Please keep the discussion on extrinsic motivation in mind. You don't want to go overboard on giving out treats and rewards, so be sure to keep it balanced.

Question six asks how you want your students to feel when they leave for the weekend. I like this question because it requires that the teacher plan for the tone of the afternoon meeting. You may want your kids to leave feeling excited about the upcoming week or possibly you want them to be reflective about what they learned during the week. You will need to mull this question around in order to choose the appropriate tasks and create the appropriate tone to accomplish your intended goal.

If you implement number seven, you will want to ensure that you have some type of tracking sheet that you can share with students. Some teachers use behavior charts. Students earn stickers for their on-task behavior and once a chart is filled, they earn some type of recognition. Sharing the students' sticker chart and comparing how they have improved is a nice way to share their success.

If you choose to implement question eight, think about television commercials and how they tease us into wanting to watch the upcoming episodes of our favorite television program. You can do this for your afternoon meeting by providing a teaser for kids on what you will be learning in the new week.

Kids love this and it creates a sense of excitement for them. It also encourages them to come back to school on time and ready to go on Monday morning.

A final note on afternoon meeting is that it should be the last thing you do before dismissal for the day. It is important that morning and afternoon meetings are the first and last thing that students do before they start the school day. This really helps to establish the tone for the day.

Final Thoughts

Better learning in our schools for our special education students requires that we foster collaboration and teamwork in our classrooms. When students feel like a part of their learning community, their achievement improves continually. This book has provided strategies that you can use to make your morning meetings engaging. Engaged students are students that are learning. I hope that the 100 strategies shared will bring many hours of learning and fun for you and your students. Happy teaching!

APPENDIX A:
Additional Resources

Children's Books
Autism and Asperger's Syndrome

Carmichael, Jodi, and Sarah Ackerley. *Spaghetti Is Not a Finger Food (and Other Life Lessons)*. San Francisco: Little Pickle Press, 2013.

DeMonia, Lori, and Monique Turchan. *Leah's Voice*. Houston, TX: Halo Publishing International, 2012.

Doering Tourville, Amanda, and Kristin Sorra. *My Friend Has Autism*. Minneapolis, MN: Picture Window Books, 2010.

Larson, Elaine Marie, and Vivian Strand. *I Am Utterly Unique: Celebrating the Strengths of Children with Asperger Syndrome and High-Functioning Autism*. Shawnee Mission, KS: Autism Asperger Publishing Co., 2006.

Peete, Holly R., Ryan E. Peete, Denene Millner, and Shane W. Evans. *My Brother Charlie*. New York: Scholastic Press, 2010.

Bullying

Bateman, Teresa, and Jackie Urbanovic. *The Bully Blockers Club*. Morton Grove, IL: Albert Whitman & Co., 2004.

Ferry, Beth, and Tom Lichtenheld. *Stick and Stone*. New York: Houghton Mifflin, 2015.

Keats, Ezra Jack. *Goggles!* 1969. Reprint, New York: Puffin, 2015.

Sornson, Bob, Maria Dismondy, Kim Shaw, and Jim Fay. *The Juice Box Bully: Empowering Kids to Stand Up for Others*. Northville, MI: Ferne Press, 2001.

Collaboration

Davis, Aubrey, and Dušan Petričić. *The Enormous Potato*. Buffalo, NY: Kids Can Press, 1998.

Pinkney, Jerry. *The Little Red Hen*. New York: Dial Books for Young Readers, 2006.

Ruzzier, Sergio. *Two Mice*. New York: Houghton Mifflin, 2015.

Diversity
DeRolf, Shane, and Michael Letzig. *The Crayon Box that Talked*. New York: Random House, 1997.

Parr, Todd. *It's Okay to Be Different*. Boston: Little, Brown, 2001.

Feelings
Bang, Molly. *When Sophie Gets Angry—Really, Really Angry. . . .* New York: Scholastic Press, 1999.

Cain, Janan. *The Way I Feel*. Seattle, Wash: Parenting Press, 2000.

Emberley, Ed, and Anne Miranda. *Glad Monster, Sad Monster: A Book about Feelings*. Boston: Little, Brown, 1997.

Tankard, Jeremy. *Grumpy Bird*. New York: Scholastic Press, 2007.

Urban, Linda, and Henry Cole. *Mouse Was Mad*. Orlando: Harcourt Children's Books, 2009.

Friendship
Brown, Laurie Krasny, and Marc Brown. *How to Be a Friend: A Guide to Making Friends and Keeping Them*. Boston: Little, Brown, 1998.

Choi, Yangsook. *The Name Jar*. New York: Knopf, 2001.

Heine, Helme. *Friends*. New York: Atheneum, 1982.

Following Directions
Binkow, Howard, and Susan F. Cornelison. *Howard B. Wigglebottom Learns to Listen*. West Jordan, UT: Thunderbolt Pub, 2005.

Kirk, Katie. *Eli, No!* New York: Abrams Books for Young Readers, 2011.

Simmons, Jane. *Come Along, Daisy!* Boston: Little, Brown, 1998.

Sharing

Meiners, Cheri J. *Share and Take Turns*. Minneapolis, MN: Free Spirit Pub, 2003.

Willems, Mo. *Should I Share My Ice Cream?* New York: Hyperion Books for Children, 2011.

Tolerance

Fox, Mem, and Leslie Staub. *Whoever You Are*. San Diego: Harcourt Brace, 1997.

Most, Bernard. *The Cow that Went Oink*. San Diego: Harcourt Brace Jovanovich, 1990.

Smith, David J., and Shelagh Armstrong. *If the World Were a Village: A Book about the World's People*. Toronto: Kids Can Press, 2002.

Teaching Resources

Autism and Asperger's Syndrome

http://www.autism-society.org

http://www.myasdf.org/site

http://theautismresearchfoundation.org

http://aspires-relationships.com/articles_teaching_kids_with_as.htm

Down Syndrome

http://www.ndss.org/resources/education

http://www.dseusa.org/en-us

http://www.downsyndromefoundation.org

Madeline Hunter

Hunter, Robin. *Madeline Hunter's Mastery Teaching*. Thousand Oaks, CA: Corwin Press, 2004. http://www.onetohio.org/library/Documents/Dr%20 Madeline%20Hunter%20Article1.pdf

Responsive Classroom

http://www.responsiveclassroom.org

http://www.educationworld.com/a_issues/schools/schools016.shtml

http://education.jhu.edu/PD/newhorizons/strategies/topics/the-democratic-classroom/responsive-classroom

Yoga in the Classroom

http://www.nchpad.org/881/5004Yoga~in~the~Classroom~~A~New~Kind~of~Education

http://www.specialyoga.com

Social and Emotional Learning

Center on the Social and Emotional Foundation for Early Learning, http://csefel.vanderbilt.edu

APPENDIX B:
Handouts, Templates, and Worksheets

All About Me

Use this sheet to record all the special details that are all about you!

My name is _____.

My favorite color is _____.

My favorite food is _____.

My favorite game is _____.

I am _____ years old.

My portrait:

Timeline

Write the person's name on the line. then write improtant events in the order in which they happened.

Important Events in _____**'s life.**

What We Have in Common

My favorite pet is:	I like to play:
My favorite dinner is:	My family consists of:
I like to eat:	My favorite book is:

Unique Me

	Same	Different
Hair color		
Eye color		
Favorite color		
Favorite food		
Favorite game		
Favorite book		

Cultural Exchange

What country are your ancestors from?_____

_____

What type of food does your family eat?_____

_____

_____

What cultural holidays does your family celebrate?_____

_____

_____

What does your family do for fun?_____

_____

_____

What type of music does your family listen to? _____

_____

_____

Rate My Day

	Morning	Lunch	Afternoon
Monday			
Tuesday			
Wednesday			
Thursday			
Friday			

Get to Know Your Character

Who is the character?	
Appearance: What does the character look like?	
Personality: What are the character's thoughts and feelings at this point in the text?	
Actions: What is the character doing?	

Character Web

Name:

Date:

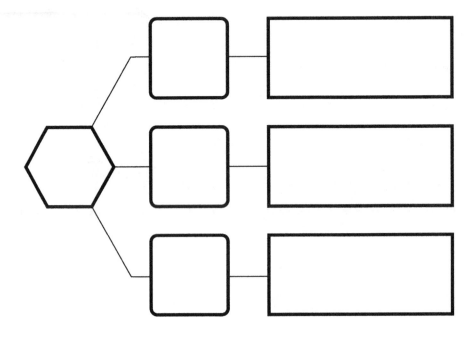

Angle Chart

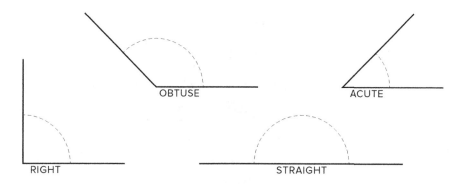

Telling Time

ANALOG CLOCK

■ = HOUR HAND   ▯ = MINTUE HAND

DIGITAL CLOCKS

AM   OR   PM
BEFORE NOON   AFTER NOON

History Detective

Event you are studying: _____

_____

3 questions you have about the event:

1. _____

2. _____

3. _____

Do research:

1.	2.	3.

Answers to 3 questions:

1. _____

2. _____

3. _____

ARTWORK CREDITS

Interior artwork downloaded from Shutterstock.com

ACKNOWLEDGMENTS

This book would not have been possible without all of the wonderful mentors I have had in my education career. Thank you Dr. Beth Bader, your continued support and encouragement has been pivotal in my growth. You were the one who encouraged me years ago to be an elementary school principal years ago.

Thank you Dr. Mary Tablada, your tutelage throughout the years has been instrumental in my writing and leadership career. Thank you for believing in my abilities.

Thank you to my wonderful family and all of your continued support. Chuck you are my biggest cheerleader and always support my endeavors. Caleb thanks for being the world's greatest son. You make me proud every day.

ABOUT THE AUTHOR

Dr. Felicia Durden, Ed.D., is an accomplished educator with over twenty years experience in education. She holds a Doctorate of Education degree in educational leadership, Master's Degree in curriculum and instruction, and Bachelor of Arts degree in English literature. Dr. Durden has taught grades K–12, served as an assistant director of reading and writing, and currently serves as principal in a large urban school district in Arizona. She has taught English composition at the college level as an adjunct instructor for over 10 years. Dr. Durden has a passion for assisting student growth for students of all ability levels.